Beyond the Empty Tomb

Encounters with the Risen Christ

Brother Richard Contino, OSF

BookLocker

Published by BookLocker.com, Inc., St. Petersburg, Florida.

Printed on acid-free paper.

BookLocker.com, Inc.
2019

First Edition

Dedication

To my mother Frances,
who has nurtured my love for Christ and the faith
and
with a special dedication of thanks
to a dear and cherished friend
Gloria Petrone
who has
become a special angel and muse whose
constant prayers and encouragement
allowed these pages to unfold.

Table of Contents

Introduction

When life presents us with either great joy or profound sorrow and perhaps especially when we become *aware of* having been bored or emotionally numbed over an extended period of time in our daily life – we might find we are particularly sensitive to our sensory perception. And so it was when I first read Brother Richard Contino's latest book *Beyond the Empty Tomb – Encounters with the Risen Christ*. It took me back over thirty years, and I found myself almost smelling again Crabtree & Evelyn's apricot-scented soap.

At that time, one month after my father was diagnosed with pancreatic cancer, my older sister was diagnosed with a form of cancer that could have proven fatal. I was on sabbatical and had nothing to do – or better said – I could do nothing, was nearly paralyzed, with these back-to-back cruel disruptions into our family's life. I didn't know what to do, but I did know that for some inexplicable reason any offensive smell was a step closer to the edge of losing a shaky semblance of order to my day. If I smelled something offensive, I wanted to swat it away with my hands. I remember passing an ashtray with cold cigar butts in it. I didn't get nauseous, but the odor crowded in on me. It lingered even when I was far away from it. The odor pulled me further into confusion and into the fear of losing my father and possibly my sister and of being utterly powerless to avoid the upheaval in my life.

One day I was shopping for some Crabtree & Evelyn soap that my younger sister liked. While looking for it I noticed some other soap – it was apricot kernel – I still remember. I smelled it and the scent was fresh and peaceful and settling to me. I bought two bars of that soap for myself in addition to the soap for my sister. The apricot soap gave off a light scent – and gave me a sense of hope, too, I guess. That scent found and settled me in the midst of darkness and confusion and offered me a path through it all into something else – I hesitate to label the "something else" because all I knew at the time was that the scent offered me something other than darkness, confusion and fear.

That particular scent is no longer on the market, but if I happen to recall it and find it on e-bay, I will buy it – I have bought it. It anchors me now. It re-places me on the horizon of having faced death, fear, darkness and so many other aspects of life I wanted to pretend did not exist – and that apricot scent reminds me that I am here now – that I came through it all. That I have learned from it – that life does hold and reveal and invite meaning and peace and joy. That life is worthy of trust.

Now what in God's name does this apricot scent have to do with an empty tomb and encountering the risen Christ that Richard Contino writes about in his new book? As I read his book I stopped circling the times he uses the words *fragrance, scent, aromatic, smell, linger, pervading, aroma, fragrant*. These words weave paragraphs and chapters into the emblematic shroud left behind in the empty tomb as testimony of our God's faithful promise that *love is stronger than death* and *we need not be afraid*. The fragrance of the risen Christ lingers and pervades the life of each person in this book. Mary the mother of Jesus, Nicodemus, Thomas, Peter, Pilate, Barabbas, Veronica, John – each of them recalling the previous three days' love, cruelty, agony, fear, hope, shame, regret, loss of meaning, loss of hope, loss of love, tenderness and harshness – as simultaneously the mysterious shining light and scent of the freshness and love of the Risen Christ creep into their daily lives and call them to the promise of our God that *love is stronger than death – that we need not be afraid.*

Our God revealed through the life, death, resurrection and ascension of Jesus is the self-emptying Love who in Jesus lived every human emotion and chose to trust through being handed over to torture, death, burial, descent into hell and ultimately resurrected into the loving Trinitarian life from which he was sent. The self-sacrificing, self-emptying love of God releases a fragrance that can only be generated through being pulverized. The Chinese written language is based upon vivid shorthand pictures, symbolic expressions, of the operations of nature. The Chinese written character for "fragrant" is made up of ripened grain that, when under the warm shining rays of the sun, releases its fragrance. Through the eyes and heart and sense of faith, it follows that when the seed is planted into the earth and dies, it grows into grain, is pulverized into flour, baked into bread, consecrated, broken and shared as the Body of Christ. Death is vanquished, and we are nurtured in body and soul through the life, death and resurrection of Jesus. We remember. We celebrate. We believe.

Brother Richard takes us through Holy Thursday's washing of the feet when Jesus obliterated all that the master-servant relationship had previously defined. Richard writes, "As each man's feet were washed and dried, kissed and embraced, the room dank with many smells and odors, was inundated by a sweet and pleasant fragrance . . ." The fragrance of humble self-emptying love is emitted each time we recall Jesus washing the feet – especially of Judas. Another spiritual writer, Ken Gire, is in harmony with Richard's fragrance refrain: *"It has been said that forgiveness is the fragrance the violet sheds on the heel that crushed it. Could there be a fragrance as sweet in all the world as that of Jesus washing the very heel that was poised to crush him?"* (Moments with the Savior*).*

Richard takes us into the lives of these people and invites us to imagine what it was like to have known, feared, been challenged by, been given hope and to have been loved and trusted by Jesus. Before and after the Garden of Gethsemane – before and after the crucifixion – before and after the burial – and ultimately after the fullness of God's promise – the resurrection. Richard offers us specifics in each of these peoples' lives. Regret, shame and fear alongside the memories and hope that such tenderness and love promised by Jesus could actually be true.

When I first met Richard in July 2013, he said something that I wrote down so as to remember after we parted company. "While learning to wait along the journey, I have discovered that it is the details that matter most and not the answer." In relating what happened to Thomas as Richard imagines him fleeing Jerusalem on the same road as those traveling to Emmaus with the unrecognized Risen Christ, we see a man immersed in shame and regret and fear – so eaten by his feelings-of-the-moment that he sees nothing else. In Thomas' feelings can we not identify all too readily how we drown in our own feelings and fail to see the reality, the graced details, of our own lived daily lives as we charge forward (or so we think) to whatever goal we may set for ourselves?

In his book that Richard prayed as well as wrote, he encourages us to be present to the details in our own lives – to the apricot-scented memories that remind us of pain and hope and replaced-recommitted trust in the promise of our God. May we become ever more aware and accepting of the fragrance of our self-emptying God of Love. May we accept Richard's invitation to trust and be not afraid. This would be the honorable way to say, "Thank you, Richard."

Father Larry Lewis, MM

Chapter One: A Mother's Embrace: Mary

The fragrance lingered in the room. Though the scent was pleasing to the senses, one could not be unaware of the essence that seeped into not just the confines of the room but literally embraced the walls, floor, and furnishings with its aroma.

The enduring presence of the abiding fragrance was difficult to ignore. Such a fragrance was a perfumed ointment, extracted from aromatic nard, precious and costly to procure. This exquisite perfume had been carried within an expensive jar of alabaster into the home, and it was indeed a proper vessel to house such a treasure. The perfume and its cask would soon become the focal remembrance of the evening. Upon arrival, the bearer of the container in moments broke the jar open before the stunned guests and poured its contents lavishly over the head of the Man reclining at the table. All were amazed by the vision of this woman, the jar, and the liquid poured first upon the head and then the feet of the reclining and amazed Man. No one halted what was transpiring before everyone's eyes. Many who had followed the Man had come to expect the unexpected, but this event was beyond the ordinary and the incredible. At the table was the Man's Mother, her eyes riveted on this unfolding drama, and such an extravagant display of affection and love would be cast by others at this table with scorn and disdain, but in her heart she was pondering its meaning and purpose on such a night.

Surrounded by the lingering scent, Mary the Mother was sitting in the same room where just days earlier there was a dinner in honor of the Son and where the ointment was so generously poured. This house where Mary, Martha, and Lazarus dwelt had become a place of joy and celebration just six days ago, but the Mother of the Son now was sitting as a Mother of Sorrows amidst the remembrance of the fragrant scent, not joyfully recalled but in profound grief and sorrow.

The Mother was mourning the loss of the Son while sitting in the home of Lazarus, the friend newly raised and reborn through the words and command of Jesus who had cried out, "Lazarus, come forth. Unbind him and set him free," and the Friend and cherished Rabbi demanded that he live again. Thus, the Man unraveled death and its grip, and all who witnessed such an event were astonished.

But in this home that had celebrated such a spectacular return to life was shrouded, almost as if the house was a corpse itself, for the Son that the Woman bore at the Archangel's invitation lay buried in a tomb, buried and soundly dead, and the mission to establish the Kingdom of God so abruptly terminated that in disgrace she echoed in her frame and body a mixture of grief, tainted not with perfume but with anguish.

The Woman, grieving but so filled with grace, sat transfixed by memories of all that had occurred. Undaunted, she held tight to the words she had heard so long before and with the beating of her heart, she repeated . . ..

Be Not Afraid!

In vigil, the Mother was waiting on this early Sunday morning, as the light of a new day was about to break. However, before the morning rays dispelled the night, the Mother was surrounded by darkness, not of a physical design but of an interior and spiritual nature, for her heart was heavy and burdened. She had been broken by death, torn apart and rent by the grief of her loss experienced at the foot of the Cross.

In this strange mixture of fading night and blossoming day, the Mother's face was bathed in a glow of exterior light wrapping her in a mantle of twilight, fringed with the rays of approaching dusk.

Into this embrace of competing lights, the Mother's face could not hide the glimmer of glistening moisture that flowed in a cascade of tears, weeping for her broken heart and the image of the Son, bound and laid upon a cold slab surrounded by an oppressive darkness for these three days that the Son was lying a prisoner in the grasp of death. In the darkness of the tomb, the Son's body, absent of life and void of breath, waited for the Father to proclaim, "Arise, my Son." The plan was well done, salvation secured, and mercy overflowed to wash a waiting earth and bathe a humanity hungering for cleansing. Grace married to mercy had broken through the darkness with the Almighty's ineffable Light.

The minutes of this new day, the first of the week, were moving slowly and heavily when measured by grief. In her arms, the Mother held the lifeless form: The Son she had nursed at her bosom so long ago in Bethlehem was lying bruised and torn, a Man defiled, heaped with scorn, and imprinted with an agony no one could have foreseen.

With the Cross a cruel and mocking backdrop, the Mother succumbed to unspeakable agony, in pain and suffering for the slain child she held in her outstretched arms. In death, the body of the Man concealed no sign of the toil that God's passion for humanity had extracted as a ransom, paid and signed in the Son's blood and sealed with the marks of the wounds.

Her tears increased in their journey down her cheeks and fell upon her breasts that once nursed him, and she craved a return to that astonishing moment in the stable, but such thoughts and dreams were to no avail as she struggled to bear the burden of her grief and the weight of the Son she could no longer console.

The Mother surrendered to her pain and profound loss in spite of the words that swirl around her . . .

Be Not Afraid!

Her body released spasms of unbridled grief and sorrow, for she was mourning the Man who would always be a Son to her.

The sun's rays breaking through clouds, the Mother greeted the rising sun with a prayer formed by her life:

"Fiat, let your will be done; I am your handmaid today, as I was in Nazareth and Bethlehem, and even now in the midst of sorrow and the mystery that is unfolding within and without, I echo with my life, heart and soul: Fiat, let your will be done. In union with the Son who voiced, 'It is finished,' I offer my own profession of faith and trust and proclaim again in solidarity and surrender: Fiat!"

At that moment when her prayer, born out of a life in total obedience to what Yahweh had ordained, and she had proclaimed by her daily Fiat, there was within her frame a sudden and unexpected elation and joy. She gave voice to a phrase spoken long ago and uttered afresh: "How can this be? This feeling of joy as I sit in the midst of excruciating sorrow, filled not with a bounty of good but the emptiness of loss." With the advent of a gentle, passing breeze she distinctly heard a whisper that offered an answer . . .

Be Not Afraid!

The Mother's body sensed something amiss, for the Woman was no stranger to supernatural sounds or for the Divine to embrace her with a calm blazing, with passion yet so deeply confounding. This grieving Mother was ailing because of her anguish and aging as the breeze and whisper combined to grant her tired frame and bones the grace to rebound with fresh vigor and vibrant enthusiasm. The Mother was pondering, as she had done for so many years, and she remembered how the Spirit overshadowed her and with her assent she grew fruitful and gave birth. What then were these stirrings, so disconcerting in the midst of unbridled anguish?

The image that she was struggling against but would not vanish from within her mind, for it was seared there with her love. The Man lying prone in her arms, the weight heavy but no burden for the Mother to bear, for she would carry the very wood they had hoisted upon his shoulders. The nails they drove into the Son's hands, the Mother would outstretch her own hands to receive to spare the Child she loved, but she knew she could not bear the wood nor take the nails, for this was the reason for her "Fiat," and the Son's "It is finished!" If she had not witnessed the tortured death beneath the wood of the Cross and had she not held in her arms the weight of His brutalized body, even she, this Mother, would hope that with the morning would come the Divine Salve, and she might awaken from such a ghastly nightmare. But alas, this was no dream, nor dark shadow of devilish delight, but the inconceivable truth, grasped in her mind and heart that the Son was indeed dead. In the wake of such feelings of a distraught heart, she pondered the tension of her grief and a consoling breeze, and listening intently she perceived a rush of grace that echoed . . .

Be Not Afraid!

The sun was rising, as Yahweh ordained each day, to bathe this room in its light, but with a difference for the Light had a celestial glow, and the Mother remembered that such a glow had come upon her when she received an Archangel as a guest. She had assented and was bathed and embraced by the fire of the Spirit and touched by a Divine kiss, as her womb, barren and still, pulsed alive with the bounty of the Divinity's love. These rays of the sun entering this room did so with such force that the solar heat, exciting the lingering fragrance, burst into a more potent perfume.

The Mother's senses were captivated by the infusion of sunlight and the refreshed fragrance that she was overwhelmed with the sensations. Swooning to her cushioned chair, she was confused by what she perceived as the twining of the physical and the spirit in union, as she remembered a similar feeling and experience years earlier when an unearthly scent filled her with joy, and on this day of desolation, she again tasted, smelled, felt, heard, and touched it. This day of misery and emptiness struggled to compete with her affections and demanded her awareness of something soaring within, and a sudden heat rising from within her soul enlivened her senses, as she perceived the whisper again . . .

Be Not Afraid!

Suddenly, the Mother's pulse quickened, the heart awakened feverishly, for her hearing was shattered by a piercing sound. Beneath her feet, the Mother felt the earth rumble and the ground sway. Yet she was not fearful but content to move from desolation to calm, a prelude to the consolation of a Visitation, a procession accompanied by a Light that overwhelmed her sight but not her hearing, for she heard the Voice utter "Mother" in a tone that she alone knew could be no other but the Son she had borne, and wondering aloud, she asked, "How can this be?" In return she heard with crystal clarity . . .

Be Not Afraid!

Through the effluence of Light, emanating outward to encircle the room, the Son, resurrected and glorious, proceeded forth to transform this quaint and tidy room into a heavenly abode.

No words need be exchanged nor verbally expressed for it was a sight alone that confirmed and then confessed and rejoiced, proclaiming that the Man of Light was the Son, her Son, and the Mother raced in bounds, leaping the chasm of the great divide, for the Son had conquered death and was fully alive!

Who could imagine the scene, surreal yet fully present in the moment? The Son was alive and standing before the Mother. Was there language to describe or emotions to identify the mingling of the divine and human love in such a moment when what was thought dead was so fully alive. Could the human mind comprehend the unimaginable or absorb the reality of what was transpiring before unbelieving eyes. The impossible became possible because God had designed a plan with the intricacy of a detailed weaving of love and forgiveness, and when expressed in its fullness, the Son stood in magnificent glory before the Woman who bore the Child, nursed the Son into manhood, and in an agony of astounding sorrow, buried the Son who is transfigured before her.

And then she heard the words . . . *Be Not Afraid,* . . . and that allowed her trembling feelings to break forth, not in a quest to understand but in a maternal instinct to embrace the Living Son. No rebuke was there for a momentary lack of belief, only an uncompromising devotion of a Mother for her Child, and in this remarkable moment the Mother who had stood beneath the Cross shared in the triumph of the One she bore as a Child, now in exaltation as Victor crowned Lord and Christ.

The embrace was exhilarating, exuberant, and intoxicating, and the Mother stimulated beyond the normal sensations of body touching body, for this was another form of experience, and the perceptions were at once unique and mysterious. An aura encircled this embrace to become a glorified form of what just days before was a grief-stricken Mother, a Pietà in profound sorrow and despair, but now exuded nothing less than unrestrained joy.

Days before when the Son breathed his final breath, the celestial heavens had been quiet and draped with a heavy pall of sorrow, but today on this Sunday there was an ecstatic union between heaven and earth, unheard of since the days of creation, and the strains of melodious exaltation chanted their glorious lyrics of "Alleluia, Alleluia, Alleluia, worthy is the Lamb who was slain; all glory and honor belong to him forever and ever," temporarily replacing the hosannas as heaven and indeed all creation sang and echoed a common theme . . .

Be Not Afraid!

"My Son, my Son" was all the Mother could express as she held him tight in a grip, filled with unrestrained joy but a hesitancy, for the Mother feared, if she let go, the Son as he now appeared would suddenly disappear. The tighter she grasped, the more light infiltrated the room that just moments before had been the center of dark gloom. Could one for a moment even imagine the encounter? One who was dead was now alive and glorified, standing before the Mother whose love without any control or impediment released a volley of kisses to match her clutching hands with a depth and hunger that only a Mother that bore the Son could unleash.

It was not passion but undignified relief that the Son she saw in such agony and held in her arms so surely dead was standing before her with a gaze that enflamed her soul and excited her mind and heart. She could not fathom the reality she was witnessing, but knew for certain this was the Child, her Son, who stood before her.

No explanation or reason was necessary, for faith alone had transfixed the gaze, and the recognition of belief that her Fiat offered so long ago had come full circle as the treasury of divine grace exploded upon the universe as a saving balm.

She touched the hands, imprinted by the marks of the nails, and she shuddered from the agony of memory. Her hands glided to the side, to the wound opened before her eyes, and she witnessed the flow of blood and water and cried for he was dead. But without any misunderstanding and hallucination of the mind, her heart could define this was the Son she had called Jesus, and now in Resurrected Glory was the Christ, the Son of the Most High.

How could this be? The question echoed again, but this time no archangel but the Son proclaimed, "Mother, it is I," and what her eyes perceived, her heart and mind gratefully assented to. And for the first time since the events of that first Good Friday, she understood and experienced the truth when he said . . .

Be Not Afraid!

Tears continued to fall, this time in a gentle manner for they were the tears of unmitigated joy, of love overflowing, and a gratitude that only tears could express, for the gift of life was standing majestically before her. Days earlier, she truly had been a grief-stricken widow, entrusted into the arms of the apostle and faithful companion, John, and today she was Mother again, no longer alone but in full stature becoming the New Eve of a New Creation. The Son's eyes gazed upon the figure of the Mother, now the Woman, for she would be entrusted with the task of giving life to the community of witnesses who from this day forward would be born and raised within the glow of this Resurrected Son and the reality of the empty tomb.

How, why, when or where no longer held any sway. Human questions must bend to the Divine Order and Command and the understanding that for those who would believe no proof was necessary, and for those who did not believe, there would never be enough proof.

But before the Mother, gazing eye to eye stood the Victor and the Son. The battle was indeed done. The victory won, humanity had been retrieved from the misery of sin and death, and the tomb no longer held such power, for the Light that was aglow attested to the saving grace that death was not an end but a transit to a more enduring life. And again the Mother and the world heard the words that had become an exuberant refrain . . .

Be Not Afraid!

Held together in this embrace, Mother and Son conveyed an image of maternal grace, a tableau depicting for endless generations the union of Divinity with humanity, made possible through the suffering that the Son endured on the Cross. In a lingering, unique and intensified supernatural motif, the experience at the foot of the Cross was a birthing anew, expressed in pain and suffering through the sacrifice of the Son, so freely offered, and graciously ushered into a style of living, once unknown because of the sin of Eve was now relieved. In that moment beneath the Cross, the dying Son, a strange and unfathomable paradox of death to life was conceived, and the Church was born. The Church, impregnated was born, and then set apart as a resplendent witness, in a sublime movement upon the earth and to all the corners and reaches of the universe. By Word and Ritual, a remarkable vision of a saved and restored world where the Son was reborn, would enthrall for all time as the Alpha and the Omega, whose Voice and Resurrected Presence would intone for all ages to come . . .

Be Not Afraid!

As a Child clothed in swaddling cloth, robed now in resplendent Resurrected Glory. Before held and bound in human form, the Son was set free, unbounded and unconstrained, for time and space held no demands but bowed to the Divine prerogative. The Nazarene, Galilean, Jew, and Rabbi had claimed the crown of the Messiah and was declared King as a new age was dawning, and the Son bore the exalted title, Lord and Savior. The Mother, herself, young and a virgin encased in innocence, was embraced by a covering of fragrance, clothing her in the scent of Divinity. She, the first virgin through surrender, became Mother beneath the Cross, and enfolded in the mantle of Divine fragrance was today and for all ages blessed among all women! Thus arrayed, Virgin, Mother and Woman for all generations would most assuredly be voiced as blessed, for this Divine embrace possessed all her form and frame to grant her stature, engraved with grace and profuse dignity. And within this enfolding and sublime embrace, she heard whispered within her ear . . .

Be Not Afraid!

Unaware that in generations and ages yet to come would be raised in her honor and for the glory of God grand and spacious basilicas where the faithful would ask in prayer for her motherly intercession and for the aid and comfort of her love and protection. In various places throughout the world would be erected immense plazas where multitudes would come to seek her favors to feed, to clothe, and to heal of the diseases of the heart and soul, as a loving Mother to her children. But foremost would be the one command that she would give to the children of the Man: "Do whatever he tells you to do." Such sage advice we should all endorse, and from this one sentiment would come what she most implored: a host of faithful sons and daughters, eager to follow the Son that she had borne and proclaims to be the Risen Lord. In ages without numbers yet conceived, this Mother, who was mortal, would transport her favors through the portal of human time and history, and from where we were standing today, the places marked forever by the fragrances of holiness would be a geography of grace for the woman of simple elegance: Fatima, Lourdes, Guadalupe, Kibeho, Czestochowa, Our Lady of Perpetual Help, Our Lady of the Miraculous Medal, Loreto, Kazan, Tinos, and countless others, for there was no land where this Lady's fragrance had not reached, not because of her efforts but because of this incredible encounter and embrace. The Son did so command when from the Cross he had bequeathed to a disconsolate people the presence of the Mother, not just for this time but also for the eons yet to come.

No longer a widow or a grieving Mother, she was the New Eve and Mother reborn, who would give birth to countless sons and daughters who would follow the Way. In this room, steeped in fragrant memory, the Virgin, now Woman, would return to the Cenacle, and there waiting in prayer, pondering, and contemplating, she would tend to her Son's disciples as they prepared to go forth as apostles. They would be confirmed and affirmed in the mission to proclaim the Good News by the Risen Son, who would breathe the power of healing and of forgiveness on them. The Mother to this extended brood, she would by her presence assure the weak of heart and by her prayer would support those who embarked upon this mission, encouraging each by her own conviction, "Do whatever He tells you to do!" and the refrain . . .

Be Not Afraid!

echoing all around as this embrace tightened, as if to make sure this moment was real and solid.

The Mother was afraid to let go, fearing that her vision was nothing more than a broken heart wishing to rewrite the pages of yesterday's history. But the Mother sensed this was flesh that she embraced and touched. Not a fanciful imagining of a distressed heart and a sorrowful spirit. The bruised flesh, although all aglow, still bore the reddened imprint where the nails had held the Son bound. The face she held so gently in her hands bore the marks of the thorns and crown that imprinted their violence upon his brow. Her hands in almost disbelief traced the reddish wounds and then cupped his face with the cherished smile she knew anywhere as the characteristic of the Jesus she had conceived, bore and bred. This was her Son she knew and believed in this morning hour; the sun even bowing to acknowledge that its light and rays were no match for the Son that now appeared to break the tyranny of darkness that held all humanity captive. This Light of the Son radiated outwards and embraced all who believed in a faith that could not compete with the rays of the sun that for just this moment had dimmed in reverence to the act to transform the world and the universe, now unbound, and set them free. When once a disobedient forefather and mother had lost the warmth, the Son in obedience to the Father reignited the degree of the Father's love to warm the universe and give light to the wandering souls. The sun and the

Son mingled with the fragrance that pervaded the entire room and house just days earlier as a gesture of love and devotion and now ignited the fire blazing as a single Light and shining so bright in the Son who pierced the darkness to reassure a grateful but unaware humanity . . .

Be Not Afraid!

The Son, dazzling in an array of raiment spun by no mortal hand for he was wearing a celestial robe of delicate and intricate strands of love, compassion, forgiveness, and mercy. The strands were bound together in a weaving of grace binding these separate threads into a robe of magnificent colors to outshine the stars and even the sun in brilliance unfathomable by human reason and dwarfed by the radiance that the Resurrected exhaled and breathed such Light and Life upon an unsuspecting but redeemed people. The Mother was aware that a garment shielded her Son's frame and was not made by her hands, but sung into being by an angelic seamstress. Its texture smooth and soft, its folds abundant and flowing. Colors abounded, shimmering and shining, and for a moment the Mother became faint with this display of heavenly delight. But ever the dutiful Son, He removed from the copious folds of his regal garment the rough linen that held his body secure when surrendered to death and to the grave. Into her waiting arms and willing hands, she received a token of God's reminder to her, the Mother who believed, and to the host of the faithful that would struggle in the centuries to come in this state of faith that each was to remember the divine response to all the struggles, clouding the heart and stifling the mind . . .

Be Not Afraid!

She recalled with a pang of horror how just days before as her Son had arrived at the hill named Golgotha how the garment that she had woven with her own hands had been ripped from his body with no small amount of brutality. She recalled the hours and days as she had collected the cloth from the sheared sheep and then with nimble fingers plied the strands that became the threads she had woven upon her household loom into the robe that the Son would wear during his days of ministry. The garment was of no distinctive brand but in the style of the lowest of men. Poor and rough in quality, however, woven with a degree of love that gave the cloth and its wearer a mark of great dignity. The cloth that became his tunic was of no great repute but woven in one full piece. It protected the Son from the heat of the sun's glare, as He strode the roads and the plains to preach to all that would hear of the salvation so near. This clothing was a special gift from the Mother who knew the day would come when the Child she so loved would leave her home to embark upon the Father's plan to announce the Good News that the Kingdom was at hand.

The tunic was a fresh reminder to the Man that the Mother's love would follow wherever his heart would lead and that she alone would be the first to believe from the moment she had conceived that the King would become a Child. The tunic was woven with care and with love, and within its fibers would blend the tears that she had shed, knowing full well as the years progressed the reason for the Child would be made manifest.

There upon that hill on that awful day when the rough hands of soldiers had torn the tunic she had woven with love and care, this garment was cast as a sign of the unique bond between Mother and Son, conceived in the phenomenal mind of God the Father so that humanity could only savor and wonder. She witnessed as that cloth of love was dragged to the dirty ground and soiled by the hands of his gruesome executioners. She watched with horror and dismay, as her body stepped forward to rescue the cloth, covered in blood and grime, and as her arms grasped what she could hold belonging to him, a man with little dignity nor concern, had rent from her trembling hands the one vestige that still claimed the scent of the Son she did so love and grieved for the pain that He had endured. With mocking faces, the soldiers who had nailed her Son to the wood would make a game of dice in full sight of the Man, securing salvation for all those grasped by human time and held bound by sin and fear, and they would gamble for the cloth that held not just the scent of this Sacred Man but the fragrance of the love that the woman had woven into the wool of the garment that the Man could no longer shoulder.

Today, however, the Son, so aware of the pain, extricated from the heart and soul of the woman He so loved that into her hands He bestowed a grateful gesture for her uncompromising devotion and dedication; a simple cloth that covered his body that He relinquished, for his coverings were of a heavenly kind to wrap the Mother with an embrace of divine acclimation. She gathered the cloth to her breast and understood the gesture as a sign, forever requested and granted to the children of man . . . that each and every generation should understand that in this moment and in their own time to listen carefully and believe . . .

Be Not Afraid!

With the cloth folded carefully and placed within a chest present in the room, it mingled with the fragrance that dominated its confines. The Son, who was anointed just days earlier, returned after a journey of cosmic proportion and universal importance. From the wood of the Cross, salvation would be achieved and redemption conceived in the mind of God, first by humbly becoming human in the womb of the Virgin, now a Mother, and then wrought to completion with a bound and deceased body, raised glorious from the ground. The fragrance mingled with the odor of resurrection, and suddenly, a sensory intoxication of sheer delight captivated the Mother; and again she nearly swoons, but the arms of the Son, so strong and renewed, embraced her in the near tumble, not from anxiety or fear but from the release of grief instantly dismissed, and in its place a new fragrance permeated the space. It was not aromatic nard but a unique and heavenly scent, a joy of a new aroma with a spirited bouquet. Such a fragrance would be necessary for the sons and daughters of this newfound Way: That a man, and not just any man, but the Man they called the Son of God, would be proclaimed as resurrected and set free was madness to be sure and most assuredly would inflict a price upon those who claimed this newfound fame. Such a folly would require the Mother to stand guard over those who might waver, and with her presence would remind all those assembled that the Son was resurrected and returned to the Father and would send us about the world to proclaim and to remember his refrain of joy mingled with hope . . .

Be Not Afraid!

With the burial cloth so secured, the Mother was seeking insight in the Son's eyes on what course this newfound life would determine for her and the others who had been scattered. He expressed in a language no longer needing words, but speaking a conversation guided from heart to heart, and in this communication invited her to join him at the table, for the morning had advanced and was in need of sustenance for the Woman who had only tears to feed upon. Seated at the table, He secured the bread placed before him, and with an adoring gaze she focused upon his face that shone with abundant grace and glory. Was this a dream that from its drama she would awaken and find in its place that grief had not been muted but made more resolute and profound? "Dispel such thoughts," her Son and Lord had implored, as she pondered all these things that filled her heart, and in a burst of tremendous combustion, the odor of the burial cloth and the fragrance of the anointing lingered, igniting an explosion that did no harm but heals the loss that plagued the heart to remind the Mother . . .

Be Not Afraid!

In a moment reminiscent of a few days earlier, the Son took the bread into his scarred hands, and raising his eyes to Heaven, called upon the Father, giving thanks for all that had been wrought by the power of love and the acts of grace. The Mother, who had spent her life in caring for the Son, waited with beating heart as he uttered with great comfort, "Take and eat, for this is My Body, blessed, broken and given, to be assured that I am with you, even to the end of time." From these hands that embraced the wood and the still-visible wounds that wrought redemption, she accepted with intense devotion the bread, no longer such, but divinely the Son Himself in a mystical union, a memorial forever bestowed, not just in symbol but in presence perpetually.

Frozen in time, this image of the Mother in a trance of devotion consuming the bread experienced the joys of the angels. On that Friday, depicted for ages to recall, remembered and commemorated was this image of the Woman and the dead Son draped in her arms, and on this Sunday, a new scene of the Son and the Mother, a table turned altar and bread transubstantiated from wheat into the Body of the Son with the Mother in a poise of gracefulness as the depth of interior devotion displayed ecstasy with supernatural affection. As her heart swooned to a melody of joy and incomparable delight, her eyes opened, and she heard the request to tell my brothers to meet in Galilee, and before she could reply, he vanished and was gone. As her eyes adjusted in the afterglow of the ethereal visitation, there was an explosion of the rare kind, for the fragrance had permeated the room and mingled with the odor of resurrection, bathing the room and the Woman with a combustion of superb wonder, amazement and joy, dispelling the darkness of death and the wails of grief, replaced by abundant Light and the jubilant chords of "Alleluia! Alleluia! Alleluia!" sounded in the vaults of heaven, for death had been conquered and sin forgiven by the Man who was the Son of the Woman who joined in the chorus of this resurrection song, ending with a final verse for the Mother and for us . . .

Be Not Afraid!

Chapter Two: A Treasured Veil: Veronica

The young girl experienced a restless night of sleep and so was rather unsteady when she awoke. What stirred her were not the sounds in the house, or the rooster crowing, but rather a scent so pleasing and fragrant that she felt enveloped by a sweet but overpowering aroma. She tried as best she could to determine the exact nature of the scent, but she could not. Her sleepy mind thought of herbs and flowers that she recalled to determine the design and nature of the fragrance that was tantalizing her senses. Abruptly as she awoke from a very dispirited sleep, her mind was busy identifying the most pleasurable scent sensation. It was not food preparation or a spice even, though she was familiar with them all since she prepared and cooked the meals for her father since her mother had died. It was not a scent associated with flowers in bloom, especially during the Passover season and in ample provision throughout the area and their own parcel of land. The plot boasted a vegetable garden but also herbs, and an array of beautiful flowers filled the house with various fragrances, but not the one that caught her attention this morning. It was nothing that she could easily remember or recall, but the fragrance was strong enough to the point of overwhelming, and yet she could not identify what the element was that so fascinated her senses. She turned her attention to the fragrance that captivated her rising, and she bolted upright when she thought she heard a voice, or rather a whisper, and she leaned in to be attentive and what her ears heard was one phrase . . .

Be Not Afraid!

She imagined she was still in a dreamlike state and so ignored what she surmised as someone speaking with her and through these words attempting to calm her heart and spirit. She knew that she was most definitely feeling and experiencing moments of anxiety, and her father had noticed the restless nights that robbed his daughter of peace. He was sensitive that her normal attitude was cheerful and pleasant, but now she was downcast and somber, causing him great concern. In fact, it was not just sleep, but her eating that was affected. These past three days had been difficult for the city of Jerusalem since the execution of a would-be messiah had caused such tension in the city and grave anxiety with the religious leaders who feared reprisals against the Temple if there was unrest during Passover.

Nathan had little care for the matters of state, but when that concern placed him or his daughter at risk, he grew attentive to the goings on at the Temple and the residences of Herod and Pilate. There had been much talk these days about this Rabbi from Nazareth as the celebration of Passover approached in the city of Jerusalem. Stories circulated throughout the region as to the Rabbi's teaching, the miracles that were connected to this Man and his large following that raised alarm in the Sanhedrin and in the halls of Fortress Antonia, as well as in the palace of Herod.

Nathan was aware of the numerous messiahs that had come forth in the last number of years, claiming the mantle of savior for the people of Israel. Such claims were often short-lived and resulted in the death of the proclaimer of the title and in the execution of the followers who would rather die than disown their leader. This Nazarean was just another in a long line of claimants to that title of messiah. Nathan was sure that this teacher and miracle worker was no more than a charlatan as were the others. His concern and fear were for the people, so easily duped by the charismatic and different. They would follow anyone who gave them bread to eat and a measure of hope for better days to come.

That was precisely the problem with the Chosen People. They lived in the past when Yahweh was active in their midst and saving them, and they looked towards the future when the Messiah would come and vanquish the enemies of Israel, returning the Jews to the glory days of the reign of King David. It was the present time that caused such anxiety and confusion among the people. The people suffered under the oppressive domination of the Romans. They felt burdened by the demands made upon the ordinary people by their religious leaders who insisted upon ritual and practices that sometimes were more tiresome than worthy of worship of the One True God. Taxes and laws placed a heavy burden upon the children of Abraham so that if someone came into their midst claiming to give them rest, they listened and obeyed.

There was much consternation in this city since the events of the weekend when this Rabbi from Nazareth was said to have raised a prominent Jew from the dead, as those who witnessed the event came to believe. Throughout the region, word spread, calling this Jesus of Nazareth the Messiah. If this were not enough to stir the level of discontent, this same Rabbi entered the streets of Jerusalem and was hailed as a King and the

Messiah by vast throngs that assembled when they heard of his travels for the feast of Passover.

Calling such attention to himself, this Rabbi and his subsequent actions would ultimately bring the force of the state to bear upon him, and finally it resulted in the order to execute him. Such actions that began with his triumphal entrance into the city were only compounded when what this Rabbi did in the precincts of the Temple turned the tide of public opinion against him, especially those of the religious and political leaders. Having entered the city to the full adulation of the people who were certainly aware of what had transpired in Bethany with the raising of Lazarus who had been dead for four days. It had sparked a crowd to wave palm branches and to hail this Jesus as a King, declaring him to be the Messiah.

Entering the city, he had accepted the grateful homage of the people and had made his way to the Temple, and upon entering, he had caught everyone unaware when he began to toss the tables of the money changers aside and to free the animals meant for sacrifice from their cages. What should be a place of calm and peace was turned into an arena of confusion and hysteria. Neither Caiaphas nor Pilate looked upon this action as religious but as an outright rebellion against faith and the state. Jesus' actions had caused a chain reaction that before the end of the week this Rabbi who had preached peace would be at the center of a crisis that would not abate until he was arrested, condemned, and then executed.

Nathan was concerned because his daughter, Veronica, was swayed easily by matters of religious piety and gossip about the coming of the Messiah. Since the death of his wife and her mother, Nathan had tried to offer his only daughter a home that was safe and secure. This Rabbi and his preaching and display of magical powers were affecting the entire nation and creating an undercurrent that was about to engulf the nation because of this one Man, Jesus of Nazareth. Nathan had forbidden his daughter to go anywhere near this Rabbi, but like any father, he knew that just like her mother, she would follow her heart, not his commands. She often would disappear in a crowd to listen for hours as this Rabbi preached.

His words and his actions touched her gentle heart, and she began to long for the days of the coming of the Messiah and hoped that perhaps this Rabbi was just that Man, as promised by Yahweh.

How everything dramatically changed when the Rabbi, betrayed, they say, by one of his own men, was arrested and placed on trial before the leaders of the Sanhedrin and condemned to death on the charge of blasphemy. Brought before Pilate for the issuance of the decree for execution, he was hung upon a cross on the hill of Golgotha, died, and buried. Nathan still shuddered when he remembered the events of that Friday, especially when he became a witness to the saga and the outlandish behavior of his daughter, who had sought to console this criminal in public view of the mob at the brutal scene of crucifixion. Had it not been for the fact that he was engaged upon the affairs of business, he would have insisted that Veronica was safe and secure at home.

Leaving to attend to business, he had advised Veronica to stay inside because since the arrest, the city was ripe with fear and saturated with intrigue. Veronica had no business in the streets this day. Knowing her concern for the Man she believed to be the Messiah, her father insisted that for her safety she should obey and stay within the secure walls and not venture into the cauldron stirring outside, so hot with anger and sizzling with fear.

Once Nathan was gone, Veronica could hear the throng, not claiming Jesus as King, but excited with the scent of blood and calling for Barabbas to be freed and their King to die upon a tree. She needed to witness for herself what was happening to her beloved Rabbi, so rejecting the safety of her secure home, she prepared to leave, placing over her head as it is prescribed, a veil when she ventured outside. In haste, she made her way through the jumble of side streets and came upon the crowd that had assembled before the place of the procurator, just in time to hear the decree of death for the Rabbi and freedom for Barabbas. How life in this city had abruptly changed in just a matter of days. On Sunday, a King, and today, Friday, nothing more than a common criminal. Life, Veronica came to recognize was fragile and so fleeting that once the forces of life intersect with the power of leaders, the life of someone like this Rabbi was of no consequence.

She caught an image of the Man who once she had waited to see and hear his words, but now before her eyes he was nothing that she could recall. Bloodied from beatings and scourging, he wore a woven Crown of Thorns that had been placed in mocking jest upon his head to inflict pain and cause him to grimace in agony. Many took great delight in all this, but those who thought he was the One stood in profound silence and sorrow, helpless to repay the Man whose life and words gave them such hope.

Standing before her and this insidious crowd, the Man who had raised Lazarus from the dead and given sight to the blind was nothing more than an object of derision and a spectacle to satiate the mob's thirst for bloody sport.

Veronica was horrified that people could be so brutal and vicious. The Rabbi had spoken of love and peace, yet they heaped upon his head an image of hate and upon his shoulders laid a beam, attesting to the violent and arrogant cruelty.

She wondered who really was the criminal that day. Jesus or us? The mob was not always outside, but sometimes it was within! In the midst of this ugly pantomime of justice, Veronica's heart broke with pain because of what she was witnessing: beauty, horribly disfigured by the cruelty of man. How the Voice of the Man was silenced because the mob was ranting and raging to crucify him! Crucify him! They could not hear the whisper and the Voice trying to reassure her . . .

Be Not Afraid!

His body and frame were no longer a testament to confident conviction and self-assuredness but weighed down by the burden of it all. He looked forlorn and so alone. She tried to cry out to assure him that she believed and would not give in to the demands of the crowd to see him dead upon a tree. Why, she wondered, would a Man who could make the lame walk and the blind see be treated so miserably. What satisfaction did men receive to treat each other so cruelly? This, she knew, was not God's plan, and this for sure was not the Master's idea of the Kingdom of God. She gazed over the crowd that had come to watch a travesty unfold, and then her heart told her she needed to do something to ease his pain. The mob, however, was unrelenting in its thirst for blood, and so through the gates this march of death began. She was swept up in this gruesome display of humanity, not at its finest but at its most wretched form, and she was distraught.

She pushed her way, with much needed strength, to follow the beam she could see over the mob, and in an instant it disappeared. She feared the worst, and from a small opening in a seam of this maddening crowd, she saw the Man had fallen beneath the burden of the Cross and was lying prone upon the ground. The soldiers were unrelenting and with no regard, they hollered for him to rise and continue this walk of shame. When he did not respond, instead of pity, the guards used their fists to beat and assault him. Aghast at such an awful sight, she felt her heart rend, and in that tearing of the love she held for him she heard the words that reassured her . . .

Be Not Afraid!

From deep within her slight frame came a gushing of indignation wrapped in a garment of courage, and she burst through the mob scene and knelt at the Master's side. The crowd hushed at such a sight and waited a moment to see what would happen. The courage that simmered within her body mingled with the love that she possessed for the Teacher. The phrase she had heard more than once echoed all around her as she heard with distinct rumination again . . .

Be Not Afraid!

And, as if moved to act in league with a powerful force, she did the unthinkable and removed her veil. When the veil was removed and her hair came into view, the crowd gasped, for this unsolicited act held no decorum and was shorn of any religious propriety. Imagine the sensibilities of this mob, so offended by the sight of a gentle woman who dared to show her hair in public. But for the brutality they had heaped upon this Man in the street, they carried no regret or wonderment that perhaps they had gone too far. Grumbling surrounded this woman, as with her veil in hand, she moved closer and in an act of incredible compassion, she wiped the face of this bleeding and suffering Man. The crowd, bent on anger and hate, refusing to be robbed of this game, barbaric and blatantly sadistic as it was.

They voiced their displeasure and forced the guards to manhandle the girl and push her aside with a level of disgust, allowing this crucifixion to advance unhindered by this foolishness of a slight girl.

Off to the side with his eyes wide open, the father Nathan ventured to see what the commotion was all about, and to his surprise and horror, he saw his dear daughter so compromised. The crowd, wild with vengeance, heaped its vulgar obscenities upon the child, and ripe for some added sport used her for brutal pleasure. The father, just in time, shielded the child who seemed dazed and confounded by the few moments that had transpired. He lifted her from the ground with the veil still in her hands, and with a volley of curses toward the maddening crowd, he steered his daughter through the streets and swiftly to their home.

On the way home she was filled with fear, not for what her father would say to her, but for the Man whom the mob was leading to that hill to kill. In her hands, she clung to the veil, now filled with grime, and she could see it was marked with the

Man's blood, left there as she had attempted to wipe his face clean. She was comforted by what little respite she had offered but uneasy that she had been helpless to do more to ease his pain. In those brief moments when the crowd was in an uproar, she had gazed into his eyes as she wiped his brow. She saw no anger or hate that she could surmise, but a glance that spoke a language of deep gratitude for the peril she was confronting, and in that instant when she and he met that day the Master did whisper to her and she clearly heard . . .

Be Not Afraid!

Once at home, the father was distraught. Trying to care for his daughter, he began to rant and rave, asking how she could be so careless, knowing that the streets were no place for a woman left unguarded. "We are surrounded by dangers, and you put yourself right at the center where life and death hang in the balance, and you could be cut down so swiftly." He asked her to imagine what might have happened had he not been there at that precise moment. The tears began to stream down her face, and poor dear Nathan was filled with remorse. Little did he know that her tears were not in reply to his screams and his fears, but due instead to the remembrance of the Man and the pain that he was enduring. She failed to give ample aid that would have truly been a comfort, and the tears were her regret for failing to wipe the face clean and offer some relief from the torture he was yet to endure.

Besides, even as Nathan was concerned for her safety, he grew irate when he noticed that the veil was soiled and well beyond any remedy for use again. "Coins," he screamed, "do not come so easily and cannot be wasted on a fantasy to wash clean every criminal that moves in the streets." She assured him she could wash the veil clean, and she raced to her room in the back where she went to a basin filled with some water and immersed the soiled cloth in it in hopes of dislodging the grime and blood. As the veil touched the surface of the water, a fragrance wafted to her nose, and she became delirious with the scent that quickly vanished as the cloth settled into the basin and was covered with water. For the remainder of the day, she and her father were silent, and the silence was broken, not by anything they said, but by midday the skies had darkened, and by three a calamitous storm unleashed its fury upon the city and that hill. In terror, the people huddled inside their homes, and the land rocked and shook in an earthquake exposing the city to its discontent as the scene of death had unfolded upon Golgotha that day. When nature had spent its own anger, the sun once again did appear, but the people stayed shuttered in fear within the confines of their homes, and they could not hear the words that came from the hill and traveled the streets where death had just claimed the Rabbi from Nazareth . . .

Be Not Afraid!

Before she made her bed that night, the fragrance that had appeared earlier came to life again, when Veronica wrung out from the basin the veil that still required much-needed repair, and before she went to her bed to rest, she hung it over a chair in the hope that by morning she could make the cloth usable again.

In the morning when she awoke from a restless sleep, she recalled the previous day and was concerned that her father would still be angry over her act of kindness. With her head spinning with memories of the Man and the distress she had felt at his condition, she was reminded of the veil by the recollection of its fragrance. Imagining to no avail what might be emanating from her bed, she progressed to check on the condition of the veil. As she moved closer to the place where the fragrance grew stronger, it enveloped all her senses with remarkable pleasure.

The material was dry but on her first look and inspection, she perceived some residue of the blood and grime present on the cloth. Such residue would make the material no longer viable for use, and she feared her father was right that it was worthless. Shades of dark color mingled with faded streaks that littered the garment became visible as she reached for the cloth.

Veronica, fully conscious of the sweet fragrance preoccupying her attention, took the cloth in her hands and began to unfold the material to its full length. As she did so, she gasped when she realized that what she had thought was a residue of blood and grime on the fabric was not. Holding the fabric to bear its full length, she found she was gazing on the image of the very Man she had thought to comfort. Imprinted was the very face of Jesus in all its detail and the brutal torment that He was enduring at the moment she had offered the veil, a moment overflowing with a passion of unadulterated compassion. This was no dim or faint image, but the full impression of this Man of Sorrow. Veronica's act of compassion was returned to her in kind as the face of Christ was imprinted on the fabric of the veil as an act of gratitude for her kindness.

She fell to her knees while holding the veil, a treasured remembrance of that awful day, but she was not in sorrow, but deeply affected by the image she gazed upon, the face of the Suffering Man before her. She registered the pained expression, etched by the blood firmly affixed to the veil, as if a mysterious artist painted it. The artist was God, and the paint was the love of Christ that ignited the portrait when Veronica pressed the veil to the face of Christ out of her love.

The sun began to rise, and the image of Veronica in a stance of adoration as she was kneeling before the cloth bearing the image of the One soon to be called Lord. Three days since the events of that awful day of sorrow, Veronica was silent and restless without proper food or rest. However, on this, the first day of the week as she was surrounded by sunlight and lifted in spirit by the fragrance surrounding her, she was mystified as she contemplated the image of the Suffering Man. She saw before her the face she had hoped would be the Messiah. Gazing over the details exposed in the morning light, she searched the fabric for the figure, embossed with intricate finesse so finely defined. Veronica, in reverence, realized that before her was the face of the Man she had come to acclaim as Lord and, when needed, as Friend.

Veronica shuddered as the image on the cloth came into focus, and she saw with defined clarity all the brutality that the Man had been enduring at the moment she had pushed her way into that seething crowd. The eyes were nearly closed and swollen from the repeated blows the uncaring guards had laid upon Him. The face was streaked and caked by the dirt and spittle that mixed with the blood flowing from his head where a Crown of Thorns, deviously plaited, sat upon his brow. The lips were cracked and bleeding, and the face that reflected only days before an image of God was nothing but a shallow depiction of what evil unchained could achieve and gain.

The image flashed into her memory and heart, the feelings of that day when she had tried with all her skill to offer the Man a caring hand. As she gazed upon the reflection, the eyes caught her attention, and she continued gazing, for the eyes were more than just an image but a reflection staring back at her in return. In a moment, all the emotions of the last few days came rushing in a torrent of tears and cries, piercing the morning quiet. Between her sobs and tears, she could barely hear the Voice that whispered ever so clear . . .

Be Not Afraid!

The tears continued to flow in a release of emotions, as the scent that welcomed her this morning grew stronger and more potent than before. It was as if this scent had developed a form and was literally pressing upon her, not in a violent manner, but almost as an embrace. As the stirring of her feelings mingled with this powerful fragrance, the light from the rising sun bathed the room in a beautiful glow. As all her senses were overwhelmed, she glanced at the image on the cloth, and almost as if in a haze, the image was replaced by an infusion of powerful Light. Momentarily blinded, she refocused her gaze, but there was no image; instead a Man in dazzling white was standing before her and voicing out loud . . .

Be Not Afraid!

Wondering if this was merely a dream or a hallucination because of the stress of the last few days and her lack of sleep, she was enveloped by this powerful Light, and she surmised that another was in sight. She felt a Presence not her own. Rising all around her was heat, and her eyes attempted to adjust to the glow altering her sight. In the midst of this awesome radiance was a form that was not so much earthly but of another kind, perhaps of a supernatural nature. No man or woman she knew could emit such a Light and encase a room with such rising heat. Her sight so entertained was about to share space with her sense of smell, as the fragrance catching her attention in the early hours of the morning would inundate her with an unbelievable sensory delight. This was no dream, she thought, or perhaps she was in the midst of a supernatural encounter. Her mind, blazing with all sorts of possibilities about this encounter, her ears heard again the phrase, approaching ever so closer while the image she saw was bending low to whisper in her ear...

Be Not Afraid!

Stunned, not from the light or the radiating warmth, but with clear recognition she realized she knew the Voice. It was the Rabbi, the Man she had hoped to console along the Way of Sorrow. How could this be? Was she delirious and going mad! Then the image before her was lying prone near her as she was kneeling, and in a brief look she saw the Man was the same as the One she had tried to heal on that awful day. The eyes were the same as the ones imprinted upon the fabric of her veil, and she reached out her arms to be embraced by the One who was coming to acknowledge gratefully her kindness to him that day and breathe upon her a blessing, uttered so clearly that she can hear and understand . . .

Be Not Afraid!

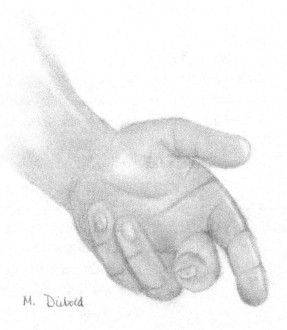

M. Diebold

Chapter Three: A Helping Hand: Simon

He rubbed his hands over and over again, just to make sure he truly was experiencing what suddenly was a very strange happening. His hands no longer ached. His fingers and joints were not just free of pain but were not even stiff, as they had been every morning for a number of past years. Each morning he had recognized the dawn only with the advent of the chronic pain that was his lot, as he grew older, and such would become his morning ritual until this Sunday.

Simon was not a man prone to complaining about his aches and pains. He was not one to pamper himself because he was aging, and his body was a constant reminder of that. He was a farmer, sturdy in build, muscles well used, and hands calloused from working the land. He was accustomed to rigorous labor, and his strong hands were his most valuable tools. However, as of late, his hands were no longer his most valuable assets. Each morning, Simon took longer and longer for his hands and fingers to adjust after a night's sleep. During the day, the rigors of his labors would cause the pain to reappear, a constant reminder of the toll that age and time had begun to take on him. By the end of a day of tilling and planting or harvesting and threshing, the bones and muscles in his hands would begin to stiffen and ache, and thus each morning his suffering would begin and persist throughout the day to such an extent that he noticed it was having an impact on his labors, which now took longer to complete, and he would lament such a state with repeated groans, audible enough for him and others to hear.

However, today he felt newborn, with hands and muscles that appeared to be those of a young man once again. Strange, for not only had the pain ceased, but his normally rough and calloused hands also were smooth and soft. Perhaps, this was all just a dream, he thought, as he sat upright in his bed.

Raising his hands to his eyes, he saw that what was normally rough, dry and calloused did appear to have been miraculously reborn during the night as new and supple skin. He raised his hands closer to his face and was instinctively intrigued by a scent that seemed absorbed into his hands, so that he rubbed them once again while gazing at them, just to confirm this was not a dream. These indeed were his hands, now fresh and fragrant, and he knew not how or why. The scent grew stronger and more persistent as his hands moved in closer contact with his own breathing, and Simon paused to savor more fully this marvelous aroma.

The morning sun filtered into the room, with the pleasing scent embracing the space, and Simon, amazed and intrigued by his revitalized hands, was jolted by a memory recalling the scent. In a flash, he remembered the scent was present during the dreadful events on Friday when a common criminal had been executed by crucifixion.

Coming from the fields as the heat of the day began to rise, Simon, like all of Jerusalem, was aware of the tensions, present and persistent within the city walls. Religious leaders were constantly on watch for any deviations from the orthodoxy of faith. Too many would-be rabbis, intent upon being proclaimed the messiah, coming to the rescue of the people were suspected and under surveillance. Of course, all of this was for the good of the people and the preservation of the nation.

Simon preferred to steer clear of this political and religious quagmire that often embroiled the innocent along with those seeking personal gain and fame. Simon, though a good and devout Jew, sought the coming of the Messiah in prayer in the quiet of his heart while he tended his fields, instead of in argumentative discourse upon the Temple stairs and porticos. As his mind raced back to that dreadful day, he shivered when he recalled the image of the Man he had somehow been destined to meet upon the streets, and in that moment of remembrance he heard a Voice saying out loud...

Be Not Afraid!

And he was overpowered momentarily by the scent, leaving him almost in a state of delirium.

Instead of becoming preoccupied with his hands, now supple and stronger than before, he took a breath and permitted himself to go back into recent memory to recall the Man. Simon was entering the gate from the outlying fields that were some distance from the city and so was feeling fatigued from the labors of the day and exhaustion from traveling by foot on his return. He realized as he entered the city, there was an atmosphere of tension and confusion, pervading this excitable city during the Passover celebration. Simon was aware, as was all of Jerusalem, of the arrival of the Rabbi Jesus, who had entered the city on Sunday. This Rabbi was no ordinary Man, for word had spread to the city limits of a spectacular event that had transpired just a few miles away. A well-known Jew and a leading member of the community by the name of Lazarus had died. Reports like wildfire spread that this Rabbi Jesus had restored the man to life after being dead in a tomb for four days. Reliable information came from well-respected men, well versed in the Torah and not given to emotional outbursts. Such news was like a flame that ignited the city into a frenzy of adulation, as the Rabbi from Galilee had entered the city. It seemed as if the whole population had gone out to greet him as he arrived for the celebration of Passover. The greeting and welcome would have been significant in any manner, but what made this both wonderful and dangerous was the proclamation of this Man as King and the declaration with definitive praise that he was not just a king, but that he was the Messiah!

Simon stayed indoors, not wanting to be a part of what was often a very changeable scene; nor was he surprised when news circulated that this would-be messiah was arrested and with rapid promptness and haste was convicted and condemned. Entering the city on the Friday before the start of the Passover celebration, he gauged rightly that the inevitable execution was already underway with Roman efficiency.

He tried to bypass the crowds streaming into the narrow passageways that would lead the condemned outside the city and to that hill named Golgotha where those Pontius Pilate had decreed should be executed died brutally upon a tree.

Simon was not a man prone to violence, nor did he have a taste for brutality. A faithful Jew, he lived the Law of Moses: love God with your whole heart, mind and soul and love your neighbor as you love yourself. Simon was a good man who devoutly followed the Law of Moses and revered not just the letter of the Law, but above all else the Lord Yahweh and the Spirit that hovered and breathed upon all. He believed in a world that should live in peace and harmony. It was Yahweh who ordained such a balance and the Law that permitted it to occur.

Simon was not a man given to sentimentality or overt religious piety. He thought of himself as a faithful Jew who prayed daily, read and studied the Torah, and observed the Sabbath and the days of feasts, especially that of Passover and the Day of Atonement. As all devout Jews, he waited in hopeful expectation of the coming of the Messiah. All hoped the Messiah, also known as the Anointed One, would free the Jewish people from oppression. These days that oppression came under the name of Caesar and was enforced with Roman armor and steel. Too often did a conqueror use the sword instead of words to placate people. The Chosen People, that is the Jews, were a special race dedicated to the Word spoken by Yahweh and preserved with devotion on scrolls. With profound reverence and humility did they unroll these sacred scrolls and read the text in order to hear and observe.

Such words as Messiah or the Anointed One entered their sacred lexicon and rested deeply in the heart, soul, and imagination of the people who yearned so for deliverance. To the Roman conquerors, such language was froth with treason and rebellion, and they sought to obliterate them, not with quill and ink, but instead used wood and nails to form a cross and frightened many into obedience to such subjugation.

Simon was no stranger to such a spectacle of Roman cruelty, having witnessed Golgotha, the place of execution, in almost constant use. Rebels, thieves, murderers, all were sent to the hill to be bound to the wood and die. This Friday was different from most displays of crucifixion for Simon would become embroiled in the parade of death as the Rabbi walked the path to Golgotha and his painful demise.

The seething crowd dragged Simon into its midst and fray, as they all saw the Rabbi fall beneath the weight of that cross. Fearing his death upon the streets instead of that designated hill, the soldiers became alarmed and pressed Simon unwillingly into a gruesome service to the suffering Man, as he was pushed into the belligerent mob and forced to lift the wood.

Initially embarrassed to the point of humiliation, Simon resisted the charge the soldiers demanded he obey. Roughed up and harshly abused, he was ordered to submit, and hesitantly, without any other recourse, he lifted the wood from the Man's bleeding hands.

Thus, this was the first time Simon saw the Rabbi's eyes, penetrating his own with a gesture that spoke of gratitude for the kindness he was extending in the midst of such barbarity. Simon felt a degree of shame, for at first he had stubbornly accepted the Cross, and the assistance had been forced and not freely given.

Simon raised the wood from the fallen Man's shoulders in the midst of this outrageous scene of terror and insanity, but when his hands touched the wood, a fragrant scent surrounded this escapade of death. With the wood planted upon Simon's broad shoulders, this walk of shame began in earnest endeavor and desire for its diabolical purpose.

Lifting the wood was not a chore or even labor for Simon. What concerned this reluctant companion were the stares the mob so disgustingly was heaping upon his frame, thinking him the criminal and not the Man. It was that scent, however, that intrigued him most. The aroma surrounded the wood and in some fashion adhered to his hands and skin. It was such a paradox that in this tumult of cries and curses, with streets littered with the putrid stench of an angry crowd, that Simon was amazed to smell such a pleasing scent. Simon ignored the crowd's malevolent taunts, and with the wood secure upon his shoulders, he walked the path with the Man unsteady by his side.

He moved at a slow pace, in spite of the soldiers' orders to be quick and hasten this grim march of death, so that at this slower speed, the man could follow more easily. With a glance backwards over his shoulder, Simon caught sight of the Man he had been forced to assist so that he might die dreadfully upon that cruel hill. All the while in the midst of this perverted exodus from the city, the aroma seeped deeper into his pores and body, and briefly he wondered why this belligerent mob did not sense the fragrance and be so tamed by the scent to embrace those with evil design.

The Man he noticed was resigned to his fate, but what seized and startled Simon was the look on his face. In spite of the savagery he had thus endured with yet more to unfold, his face was not marked by anger or rage but encased in some sort of glow that reminded Simon of the word Shalom. Once again their eyes met in an exchange of compassion, though surrounded as they were by the madness of such cruelty. Forced to continue his toil to that hill, Simon was freed of the burden once he arrived. He moved to the perimeter that the soldiers had maintained and watched with horror as the Man was stripped and then attached with nails violently to the tree.

Fleeing in sheer terror from what he was seeing, Simon heard from the now raised cross as he glanced backwards to perceive the Man utter so clearly . . .

Be Not Afraid!

For days since that dreadful moment, he had stayed hidden until this Sunday morning when he discovered his hands were once again youthful and strong. As he stared at his hands, so newly born, he recalled all that he had witnessed just days before. But on this Sunday, he felt the warmth of the rising sun heating the aroma to an intensity of sensation, and greeting this new day, he was blinded by a force of descending Light, embracing all corners of the room.

In the midst of this enveloping Light, an image appeared, and Simon recognized the face of the Man whom the Cross should have secured, but here he stood, bathed in abundant and extravagant Light. Simon recognized the eyes that spoke with a piercing gaze of gratitude on that awful and bloody day. These eyes now rested upon Simon, and with words spoken and uttered with a smile, Simon heard with delight and belief . . .

Be Not Afraid!

Chapter Four: Now I See: Longinus

He had sat in the same room for the past three days. He had been startled by the events of these days, and so he had withdrawn here, frightened by his encounter with a remarkable Man and an incredible miracle. Longinus was not the type of man, easily prone to sentimentality. He was not one to swoon or experience emotional outbursts or to give himself over to the vapors of sudden fantasies. He was a Roman centurion, molded into a soldier by the stern and disciplined tradition of the Roman legion. Loyalty, courage and discipline were the virtues that each soldier was to embrace and the standard to uphold and live. Love, religious piety, and devotion to any other deity, except that of duty and to the person of Caesar, were frowned upon with intense disdain among the ranks of command.

Longinus was Roman through and through. Hardened by years of training and campaigns, he had been brought to the far-flung reaches of the empire, and it had matured him through a tough regimen of practice and engagement. These engagements of battle, whether to put down a spark of rebellion or to secure the frontiers from the barbarian hordes, impressed upon the man and the soldier the savagery of war and the exhilaration of victory. Since his earliest days as a young boy, he had been admitted into the legions of Rome and had followed the tradition of his family lineage to rise to high status of rank and command.

Seasoned by battle and the use of the sword, Longinus faithfully responded to the command to vanquish the enemies of Rome. However, when confronted by the use of such brutal and ferocious force, exerted without restraint upon the oppressed people who had no swords or recourse, Longinus' resolve faltered. As he witnessed this cruelty and slaughter, his own heart would ache and grow burdened, filled with sadness for the suffering that had been wrought upon so many others. An enemy of Rome was given no mercy, and those who had wronged Caesar, whatever the charge, would suffer. Suffering was what was paid, and one's life was forfeited for what was owed.

Longinus was well aware of the brutality inflicted upon those Rome conquered and oppressed. The centurion understood such cruelty was to satiate soldiers' boredom, rather than to ensure the empire's security or safety. This concern for the empire was matched by an equal consideration for his men's safety, which was always his main focus. As a centurion, he could achieve more with a forceful word and his bearing than with any raised sword.

The empire was often heavy-handed when dealing with people that had been conquered and refused to be compliant to the new world order. Judea was no different from any other nation subservient to Roman rule and authority. The empire had already accorded consideration to the Jews to maintain their religious leadership, law, and worship. Such accommodation was unthinkable but for the people of Judea who considered themselves Yahweh's Chosen People. Such a relaxation of authoritative rule was a minor compromise afforded so that there would be peace.

Any hint of rebellion or treason was dealt with harshly in light of this accommodation. Jewish religious leaders were usually quick to resolve such matters so as to remain on the good side of the authorities. This political dance, so to speak, allowed the Jewish people to remain intact as a people so that they might continue the tradition and practices of faith and worship that had existed for several millennia. All involved in this intricate relationship began to unravel with the arrival of a prophet by the name of Jesus of Nazareth.

Longinus did not see the notion of an Anointed One who would set the people free as a brazen act of treason, but when this Jesus from Nazareth came into the city of Jerusalem and people proclaimed him Messiah and King, then discontent and anxiety split the relationship of the Sanhedrin and the Romans. Such discord could cast only a dark light over the people who prayed for and desired freedom.

Events moved quickly. Longinus, as he sat in his room while thinking of the events of the last days, was trying to make sense out of the fact that a Man had died horribly under his command, for Longinus was instructed to carry out the execution of this would-be Jewish king and Messiah with precision and speed. The case was not clear-cut. The Man, a Rabbi and Healer. What harm could he do to Rome or what threat was he to Caesar? Trying to understand the events that had transpired, Longinus sat in his room with a miracle unfolding. As he used his new sight to take in the breadth and depth of the room, he sensed a fragrance pervading it and realized he had experienced that same scent on that hill as he stood guard and watched the Man slowly die. With the scent in his nostrils, he was sure he heard a Voice utter . . .

Be Not Afraid!

A practical man, trained to look at the facts and make decisions not on intuition but on well-planned calculations and deliberations, he faced an odd assortment of facts. Three days ago, Longinus was blind in one eye during the execution of that Man on the Cross to demonstrate Rome's authority, and when he was decreed dead, the centurion raised his spear to pierce the side of the deceased, and what flowed from the Man's side but blood and water, which his eye had received. This bathing of the Rabbi's sustenance was enough in just a few seconds to restore his sight and change his life. With the world all trembling when the Man died and surety of foot no longer secure as the earth quaked, Longinus testified that this truly was who he said he was, the Son of God, and even in the midst of that strange afternoon upon the hill with the earth in tumult and the people filled with fear, Longinus could gaze upon the bowed head of the Man whose Heart he had just pierced without impaired vision but with his sight fully restored. In the midst of so many distracting visions, as family and friends grieved and soldiers struggled in the aftermath of the criminal's death, the inner turmoil of the commander-in-chief was lost in the disorder of the unseemly day, which suddenly grew into the darkness of night. So preoccupied were they, they could not hear the whisper of the wind saying to Longinus as he gazed at the Man on the Cross . . .

Be Not Afraid!

The soldiers quickly lowered the dead men from the crosses for the three, who had been crucified that day. A fragrance drew the attention of Longinus, as the body of the Man whose Heart he had just pierced was taken down from the Cross. One would d could imagine that the odor of a body, just deceased and bearing the signs of a convulsed and painful death, would be distinct and offensive. However, there was no odor, no smell nor whiff of death, but a pleasing fragrance spreading over the wretched hill. Jesus, the Rabbi who was accused of blasphemy and rebellion, had died quickly, but the other two suffered more pain as their legs were broken in a final agony leading to their demise. What stayed with Longinus was how they died. The Rabbi, crucified so viciously with nails to fasten him to that tree, uttered no vulgar sounds or curses for those who maimed his body. As the Cross is raised to its final resting stance, placing the body in such excruciating pain and contorting its form, the Man, when at last he raised his head, voiced not hatred but forgiveness.

From the Cross, now planted as a disfigured tree, he uttered, "Father, forgive them, for they know not what they do". Intrigued, Longinus drew closer to hear what else he would say, and he detected the fragrant scent, a mocking reminder of the ugliness engulfing all around. With the scent noticeable only to him, Longinus deemed that never before in battle or in execution had he ever seen such a manner of death. This was no charade or feeble attempt to play the crowd. The Man in dying was authentic in his unrehearsed statement coming from the heart and attesting to a life lived with intent of spirit and love. Stunned, the centurion had never before witnessed such an act so grand and so humbly selfless. In the midst of profound suffering, the Man had offered a phrase of forgiveness for the cruelty they were inflicting. No anger, no hatred, and no belligerent calls for vengeance, just sheer and unrestrained love. In a gasping Voice, the Man used what little strength and breath he still possessed to cast upon the winds the pearl of human compassion, offering to the unknowing the embrace of forgiveness for a deed so heinous. With those words just spoken, Longinus recalled the contrasting examples of the two men crucified with him. Both criminals were consigned to the cross for offenses committed and fully paid with blood and flesh. Surrounding these two crosses was no fragrant scent but the odious smell of evil and hate. The state was satisfied, and the crowd satiated with their ranting in the throes of death, but between them in the center was the Man, whose body, though broken, spoke a language of dignity that Longinus began to admire although the crowd seemed deaf to it.

In the turmoil of their dying, one of the criminals had a premonition that perhaps the Man in the center was who he said he was. Believing the opportunity for grace and the window to eternity ajar, the criminal on the right asked the dying Man, "Lord, remember me when you come into your kingdom." Longinus, intrigued, moved closer to hear the exchange and was greeted by the Man's response: "This day you will be with me in paradise." Longinus realized the fragrance that permeated the Cross in the center spread to embrace the criminal. The centurion's mind raced in a thousand directions, trying to make sense of the realities that he was experiencing and witnessing: goodness and love destroying evil and hatred. He wondered how this could be. With such assurance guaranteed, the criminal showed his relief and waited for the moment when eternity would replace the cross and with judgment bypassed through the gracious consent of the Man granting his wish to restore what was broken and repaid by the Man's blood.

Longinus realized that far more than human words were spoken here, as he sensed an implied regal authority in them that in spite of the cross, there was a throne, the nails were the scepter, and the thorns a crown. Before him he saw and heard the voice speaking with clarity and truth, and once again Longinus heard, not in a whisper but from the raised head of the Man he was gazing upon, utter in distinctive syllables through blood-soaked features what seemed only Longinus could hear ...

Be Not Afraid!

The centurion shamed by his authority and the duty that he was forced to fulfill. He witnessed the lifeblood drift from the Man who had proclaimed forgiveness and hope, amid an atmosphere of sweet scent flavoring all that the centurion had witnessed. He knew not where to look for he was embarrassed, and his uniform could not shield him from the crime. Innocent blood, he had assisted in shedding, and he was grieved. He moved away from the Cross, but his eyes remained riveted upon the Man. He could focus only partially; physically, he was disabled by a battle injury and scar and had the vision of only one eye. But with that diminished sight, he could focus from the Cross to the woman, standing as a witness to the travesty committed. It was the Man's mother, for sure. Layered in widow's garb, she was to lose the Son and forever be an orphaned mother with no child to bear, nor one to raise and call her own. As the Son upon the tree raised himself to full dignity, he addressed the mother in words that broke Longinus' heart, and tears streamed down his own face when he heard the words: "Mother, behold your Son; Son, behold your mother." He could not endure more, so he attempted to flee, but again the Voice uttered for all to hear: "I thirst!" Longinus felt a deep pang of guilt as the Man they had crucified asked a favor from his executioners: to quench his thirst. He motioned for a soldier who raced for a spear and placed a sponge soaked in wine on it. By raising it, they could make an offer of human compassion.

Longinus, his eye riveted to the Cross and the drama unfolding before him, began to notice the fragrance growing stronger with a pleasing scent, while the unfolding scene remained disturbing and foul. All around noticed a startling change in weather as the wind increased in velocity and the skies, sunny and clear a moment earlier, grew ominously dark and unsettling.

The Man tasted the sponge soaked with wine and then in a struggle to speak uttered in a gargled tone but with strength enough for the words to disturb any who listened: "My God, My God, why have you forsaken me!" The earth began to quake, and the people who had come to witness the deaths of the men, so they might gawk and mock them, became frightened as the hill moved without recourse and many lost their balance and fell to the shaking ground. Lightning flashed, and the noise of pelting rain, trembling earth and lightning strikes perturbed even the usually calm Longinus, who commanded his men to stand bold and firm and show no fear. The Man, so exposed to the elements of nature, raised his head and in a cry so all could hear above the din, "It is finished. Into your hands, I commend my Spirit."

Longinus watched as his head fell to his chest, and the Rabbi breathed his last.

From deep inside his own being, unable to control the emotional experience of the moment, Longinus cried out, "Truly, this Man must indeed be the Son of God." This confession of faith, professed to the maddening skies, released within Longinus a desire to end this tragedy. As the soldiers moved to break the legs of the other two criminals, Longinus to show the dead Rabbi some dignity would not allow them to break his bones. In a final act that would become the centurion's moment of baptism, he took the spear and lanced the side of the Man. The outpouring of blood and water completed the sacrifice as it mingled with the deluge of rain, drenching the Roman with the blood of the Man. Wiping his face clean and clear, he was stunned to realize that he saw far better than before, and the eye of no use because of past battles saw fully beneath this Cross. He understood now that this was no ordinary Man. Shocked and stunned by this reversal of misfortune, he remained within his rooms, unsure of his course of action. He tried to understand who this Man was and heard in a deep, resounding Voice, almost a command . . .

Be Not Afraid!

With his eyesight restored, he was confused when out of thin air a cloud of great Light descended within his space. No matter where he looked, the Light was so overpowering that he had to close his eyes, and as he opened them and tried to adjust to the new scene, the Man he had witnessed die on a tree appeared out of a cloud of immense Light, and in that remarkable moment he saw clearly the Man in radiant glory. Longinus, a soldier now on bended knee, cried out, "Lord I can see," and the Man of Light embraced the newborn in faith, who would become a faithful companion because he had seen and now believed. Embraced by the radiance and the Light, he was able to sense now the scent of the fragrance pervading the room, hearing again the calming Voice . . .

Be Not Afraid!

Chapter Five: The Upper Room: The Apostles

The doors were bolted and the windows tightly closed to the outside noise and light. Inside huddled ten men in various stages of disarray and states of despondency. Though the space was crowded, the room was eerily quiet. Each of the men sat in the physical quiet, but their minds were cluttered with a chaos of noise and shouting thoughts, horrible images, and accusing regrets. These last few days had been nothing less than nightmarish. These men once called by name by the Rabbi that now lay dead in a tomb as they cowered in shame and fear in this upper room. The dead Rabbi was the reason for the fear each was experiencing to varying degrees. The shame was their own, belonging to each of them, for at a crucial moment when the Rabbi needed them most, they had fled and left him alone to be captured and imprisoned.

This certainly was an incredible week, and the men grieved the loss of the Man who had called them friend. Just days ago, they had sat together in this very room to share the Seder meal and to celebrate Passover. Over the last three years, the Rabbi and these chosen twelve apostles had traversed Israel. He was the One they had all sought. This Jesus from Nazareth was the One they were convinced was the Anointed One, appointed by Yahweh to be the Messiah. They had left all. They dropped their nets into the sea and left their boats at the coast. Families thought their sons and husbands were mad as they followed this carpenter-turned rabbi from town to town, proclaiming the coming of the Kingdom of God. A tax collector, Matthew by name, abandoned his lucrative enterprise to give his wealth away and become a follower of this Man from Nazareth who spoke words never heard before in a manner unlike any teacher past or present. Some of the twelve were common folk and fishermen, and others known observers of the Law and Jewish customs, but all shared a common task. This task was to follow the One that spoke about a new law of love and the coming of the Kingdom of God in their own time and age.

This was an exciting time in the life of the Jewish people, for a fever pitch of enthusiasm for preachers and teachers reminded the enslaved and oppressed people that they were still special and chosen. Zealots agitated the people to rebellion, and prophets and rabbis called them to deeper faithfulness to Yahweh and the Law. Into this rumbling mix of faith and waiting, a man by the name of John entered this volatile scene, and with water called upon the people to prepare the way for the Lord. That way was cleared for the Rabbi from Nazareth, who came to the shores of the Jordan to begin his mission. With the words, "Repent, for the Kingdom of God is at hand," twelve men began a journey from the River of Jordan into the desert, and at the shore of Galilee, they would be called his first disciples, but now they were hiding, for the Man who had been their hope was dead.

Together, they celebrated the Passover as a family: the Teacher and Rabbi and the company of faithful disciples. While the surrounding atmosphere was explosive this Passover, for many perceived their Master a threat to the common order and good and even suggested he should stay away, they joined him as he journeyed to Jerusalem to face whatever the outcome. The outcome that transpired was the brutal slaughter of this Rabbi, Teacher and Friend by hanging Him on a tree on the hill, now called Calvary throughout the ages. Before this execution, the Master would give his pupils a final and dramatic lesson they failed to understand until the events upon that hill came full course and the Light of Grace would illumine their minds and hearts.

Hiding as they were in that upper room, each with their own thoughts, many were remembering with detail and precision all that had occurred, especially the peculiar event that transpired before the actual feast. Before the meal, the Man whom they called Master and Teacher had risen from the table. He removed his outer garment, and as the men watched a little perplexed, the Rabbi took an apron and tied it around his waist. Taking a bowl and a pitcher filled with water, he knelt and with a towel began to wash the feet of the astonished men assembled for this special feast. In stunned silence and with gaping mouths, they watched as the Rabbi took each man's feet and in gentle and loving movements washed, dried, and kissed each foot. As the water was poured to cleanse the feet, a scent began to spread, becoming apparent to all present. The Master, now clothed in the garment of a servant, moved slowly and deliberately from person to person. The apostles, these chosen few, were accustomed to the Master performing something out of the ordinary. They had heard words expressed, unlike any other by a rabbi they had known. They had witnessed the Master calming storms and feeding thousands with only a few pieces of bread and fish. They marveled when they saw lepers cleansed and sight restored to the blind. These simple men who had journeyed three years with the Teacher had seen miraculous sights, but that night before his death they were speechless when he knelt, and with love and in deep humility, did the unthinkable by washing their feet, as a servant would do.

Moving from man to man while carrying the basin and pitcher, he offered with a tenderness that only a loving father could express, the ultimate lesson of what he was expecting from them as his chosen followers: "Do as I do and be tender and loving with one another." As each man's feet were washed and dried, kissed and embraced, the room, dank with many smells and odors, was inundated by a sweet and pleasant fragrance, mixing with the smells of the assembled produce for the Passover Seder. With each pouring of water, the scent grew stronger and hung, not in an odious form but almost as a whispering fragrance carried on a gentle breeze. It touched everything in the room, and everyone began to notice the scent as if it were an embrace that encircled the room and framed its confines for the spectacular moment yet to occur.

In the midst of this Sunday morning, each of the remaining apostles, hiding from the glare of the rising sun, continued to remember that night not so long ago. The fragrance hung in the air, clinging to the room almost as an indictment of the men, so foolish on that solemn and fateful night. The scent was still so appealing on that Passover night, when Jesus their Teacher came to wash the feet of Judas. Unknown to the man, who would forever onward be called by the ignoble word, traitor, shrank in horror as the Master approached. Eyes fixed on the man who would betray him, Jesus took each of the would-be traitor's feet, removed the sandals, and washed the dust and grime from them. Feeling the water and the touch of the Master's hand, Judas allowed tears to well up in his eyes and stream down his face. Now forever the infamous traitor, he glanced at his Master and Lord and noticed that upon his face also were tears. And in a whisper ever so slight, he imagined hearing the words . . .

Be Not Afraid!

His servant task completed, Jesus, to the great dismay of his closest followers, rejoined them at the table and said so mildly that one of their number would betray him. Aghast and dumbfounded, they each asked in bewildered speech, "Is it I, Lord?" To the one who would betray the Man, he gently offered the key, "Go do quickly what you need to do." Without a backward glance, but with his head held downward, the man who would betray the King on this night of Passover when Yahweh ransomed his people, would see God prepared to hang upon a tree this night to set all of us free. As the man who fled from the fragrance and scent clinging to his cloak, raced from the room to the appointed place where evil would delight in betrayal. The announcement given, the meal proceeded with a dramatic twist that no one could have foreseen. Clothed once again in his own tunic, the Master sat at the table to celebrate the freedom and peace of the Jewish people, but in a departure from the prescribed ritual of Seder practice, he took the bread, blessed and broke it, and then to his assembled disciples, he said, "Take this and eat, for this is My Body broken and given for you."

Each of them took a morsel of bread with deep reverence and a sense of solemnity, for this was the New Passover.

Theologically, it was a new covenant, replacing and fulfilling the Old Law, and spiritually, ritualistically, and personally, for the Rabbi would become a sacrificial Lamb, a perfect, unblemished offering to atone for the sins of all. With the last morsel consumed, the fragrance grew heavy and thick as incense was rising to praise the Lord as if this nondescript room were the Temple, and the odor of sacrifice, pleasing to Yahweh.

Sitting as if in a daze and not fully understanding, the apostles three days earlier watched as the Lord who was their Teacher stretched their minds even further. Taking the cup of wine at table, he gave his blessing and passed it to each of them to drink. Widening the scope of a divine embrace, Christ, their Master and Lord, offered in a measured and confident tone: "Take this, all of you, and drink from it for this is the chalice of My Blood, The Blood of the New and Eternal Covenant, which will be poured out for you and for many for the forgiveness of sins." The chalice passed hand to hand from one apostle to another, none fully realizing what had just transpired for the veil of God had been lifted and those who were human had tasted Divinity!

Astounding as all this might be for their minds and hearts to absorb, the apostles confined these days past by fear to this upper room were haunted by the images of the pitcher and basin, still visible, and the cup and remnants of the meal present and undisturbed upon that same table. Transfixed in their minds and searing their very souls was the memory of the Master bending to wash their feet and this same gentle Man brutally taken while they slept in the garden. The scent so prevalent on that awesome night still mingled with fear and guilt as these men in shame were in hiding.

The big fisherman, the one they called Simon, held his face in his large hands, unable to look any longer at the table in disarray and haunted by the words he could not erase. For on this incredible night, when the Passover was celebrated and the words were thus changed, the Master informed him not to be so brash for he would deny that he ever knew the One he now called Lord! True to form, as the Lord foretold, he denied in arrogant and brutish form for the sake of his own skin that he knew the Lord. Not once, not twice but three times did he forsake the claim of apostle and friend and now bitterly wept these three days hence. Each morning, as the rooster crowed, the agony returned.

In this darkened room, three days hence, the remains of the meal so full of promise, lay upon the table that had been transformed into an altar. The plate that had held the bread still clung to a parcel that had been blessed, broken and given. It remained a remembrance that they were called to ponder. In the midst of the ritual, he said, "I am with you always. Do this in memory of me!" As this hidden remnant gazed upon that plate and the cup, they sensed a whisper and heard a Voice, familiar but impossible to believe for the Master they knew was dead and mute. Yet each heard . . .

Be Not Afraid!

A glimmer of light escaped from beneath the bolted door, bathing the fearful in the room in an aura of warmth, igniting with intensity the scent they each recalled. It was the same scent that bathed the room when Jesus washed their feet and gave a new command, "Love one another as I have loved you." The scent grew stronger and stronger, and many looked all around as if something was touching them. One of the apostles remembered that it was this fragrance, as appealing as the night in the home of Simon the Pharisee, that they smelled when a woman anointed the Master's feet in extravagant fashion.

The fragrance was quite evident when approaching the table where the bread and wine became more than food but a divine and sacred gift of remarkable nourishment, surrounded by the mystery of Divine Presence embraced by the common and ordinary bounty of wheat and grapes. This food no longer was just for gods, but for the men and women who would believe and understand fully that what was no longer what was seen, but what faith and heart could alone perceive.

Simon, grieving over his words spoken and the denial conceived that had harmed the Master he had confessed to love dearly and gladly give his life for, realized he was becoming distracted by the scent and the Light filtering through the door's openings, leading to this upper room. The Light seeped through cracks, visible in the closed shutters each hoped would protect them from the evil that lurked outside. The Light became stronger and so unrelenting, it could not be stopped by the doors and the shutters shut tight to prevent those inside from seeing the fear etched into each face. Although the windows were closed and barred, a radiant Light filled the room. Not sunlight, which they could clearly see, but a Light of astounding volume that filled the room with a dazzling brilliance that Simon took more than just note but remembered when he saw such a Light not so long before. Before the days of trial and tribulation that would be called the Passion of the Lord, before the Master set his face towards Jerusalem upon a Mount called Tabor, did he invite the three to see the Lord in All His Majesty. The face that was a mix of fear and despair, now all aglow, for he recalled and remembered and remembers this Light was no sunlight but a messenger of grace and hope.

At once, all those crouched and hiding leapt to their feet as the door no longer held back the onslaught of Light, reeling in waves to drown the room and all those within in the midst of this incredible scene. Did they imagine witnessing the Master in form and space, appearing before them and bathed in a spectacular transparency with filaments of Light, almost blinding to those who would look full force on this wondrous delight. He was no ghost or figment of imagination, but in flesh and spirit, light and color, dazzle and brilliance: the Master they each knew but without the words to form because eternity had transfixed the moment, and they attempted to see and believe and then to hear the words so clearly that their hearts were set free . . .

Be Not Afraid!

M. Dubois

Chapter Six: On the Road to Emmaus: Disciples

Morning had yet to break through the fabric of the darkness, hanging like a pall as the Sabbath attempted to flee from what this city had witnessed. Into this somber blanket covering every street and home as a heavy veil to suffocate nearly everyone and everything within its reach. Two men were racing to broach this mysterious and oppressive covering that wrapped this city of prophets in a shroud of sadness, grief, and fear. Such a covering caused the two to gasp for air in the stifling atmosphere, and in their anxious state they could not hear the Voice speaking in a gentle tone so as to reassure . . .

Be Not Afraid!

As the morning sun attempted to rise and break through the oppressiveness, the two rushing men reached the gates out of this dying city, and in the light of the day could be discerned the color of grief etched on these men's faces, for the words just gently spoken had not as yet been fully understood.

In silence, they made their exodus from this place of such sorrow and death and decided to travel to a town, not the Promised Land, but for each a hasty retreat and a dwelling of refuge. Emmaus was the determined course, as the men attempted to escape Jerusalem and return on the beaten path they knew so well to the place they called home. Morning now clothed the expressions of intent and stern faced men, once disciples of the One this city of Jerusalem just crucified, buried and declared so very dead. In their haste they were so preoccupied with the pace they could not hear again the Voice that attempted to slow their gait but the sounds of departing and racing feet trampling the path clamored with a different sound so they could not hear . . .

Be Not Afraid!

Preoccupied but fully aware, disciples no longer but orphans for sure, for the Master was gone that much was clear. They were lost children, forlorn and in despair, verging on being inconsolable and without any respite from fear. Stoic men, they hid their feelings deep, but their faces wore the lessons of grief. Tears were left unshed, and no words passed their lips to share as they buried deep such feelings and emotions, fearing to give voice in grief.

Sadness lay heavy on their shoulders and slowed the pace. Lost in a tumble of many thoughts, they were unaware of the stranger that approached. It was not the Man but the fragrance that caught the older man's attention. A pleasing scent that dispelled the day's gloom and lightened the weight of a heart overwhelmed by grief. Cleopas, as he was called, noticed the smell surrounding his gait. Unsure, he glanced around to determine its source and noticed the Stranger advancing towards them. The sun now risen, fully distorted his vision in a haze and glare of light, prohibiting him from seeing the Man, all in white, along the path that these three men unexpectedly shared in a surprise encounter. Distracted by the intensity of the light, neither men could perceive the form or detail of the One who was approaching, nor as they were preoccupied and distracted, could hear the voice that was speaking to reassure and calm them:

Be Not Afraid!

The fragrance was potent and rather sharp as the Man intervened on the path of the traveling pair. It was a scent pleasant and almost a balm meant to be consoling and healing for our travelers who had unknowingly entered upon a pilgrimage of hope. The One who approached was aware that their hearts were weary and sensed that their inner spirits were broken and in need of mending. "Shalom," they hear, as the Stranger greeted our downcast pilgrims, intent on solitude and silence in their grief. Their faces bore the mark of their loss. Each held a look of anxious confusion and fear, but this failed to deter the Stranger's zeal to converse about the day's affairs. The scent did not disappear nor dissipate, but with the Stranger's appearance, it enveloped the pair, now a trio, in an aura of compassion blended with an embrace of much needed mercy and solace. The men desired to keep the solitude of the day in silence along the way.

The events of the past three days had overwhelmed the hearts that did so love the gentle Master, who was brutally slaughtered, hung upon a tree, barbarically assaulted, and now dead. The memory of the Man required their reverence and shared grief, and the two travelers preferred not to be imposed upon by a Stranger who was seeking companionship and the retelling of the events and news, witnessed by these two men so painfully as they fled the city to escape its memory and the vise of its grasp.

Their trek moved forward with the Stranger taking the lead in the center in the pace and tenor of their conversation by inquiring about the reason for the haste, along with their somber faces and despairing gestures. His companions looked incredulous at the Stranger who appeared to be a friend. "Do you not know what has happened?" As those words were voiced, the two travelers were distracted from what was expressed and because of their annoyance they could not hear the subtle but distinct strain in the words,

Be Not Afraid!

Surprised at what they now shared, the elder man related an incredible but sorrowful tale, as the Stranger, seemingly more of a companion, listened intently as the pilgrims joined in the rhythm of the journey before them. He listened with intensity to the words Cleopas was speaking, with a fragrance sweet and robust surrounding their every step, as if the dust they displaced in their walking was releasing this scent. Such a scent was indeed potent and so pleasing, seeming to adhere to the white tunic the Stranger, now Friend was wearing. As the tunic flowed freely in the morning breeze, the scent was rising fragrant and strong, delicious to the senses. Fresh air, an embracing breeze, an intoxicating scent, and the soft features of the One who joined them on their walk, prompted the two disciples to slow the pace. Again, distracted by so many elements that graze the senses, they were not yet tuned to hear what was voiced upon the breeze,

Be Not Afraid!

As the tale of the One they had called Master and Lord continued to be retold by Cleopas as an unwelcome tragedy for its stark outcome. They thought He was the Messiah, and as the word was voiced, the fragrance, pleasing but unknown, grew stronger and almost touchable. Both men, looking at the Stranger whose name they knew not nor dared to inquire of, were momentarily blinded as the sunlight cast the Stranger in a glow so vibrant they must shield their eyes from the brilliance and abundance of light. Thus blinded ever so briefly, they listened as the Stranger began to speak.

His Voice, unique and not of this region, was speaking words that were calm and laced with dignity. He spoke as a Stranger, but His words were familiar and comforting. Cleopas and his companion, Rufus, were no foreigners to the words of the prophets and the Torah that this Man was using with such ease and confidence. This Stranger, now Companion, was quoting verse and line of sage and sacred wisdom from the pages of Genesis to the Prophet Isaiah, recounting Yahweh's plan to save and to heal the distraught and stumbling humanity. The men listened attentively as the pages of the scrolls began to unfold almost in thin air as the Man proclaimed and retold the story that they each knew, but somehow He was weaving it with a different thread and spinning the words of Moses and the prophets into an extraordinary tapestry for their sight to see, their hands to feel, and their lips almost to taste.

As he spoke the words, retelling the story of a people waiting to be set free, Cleopas and Rufus began to feel and sense a new energy, as if awakened from a sleep laden dream. The words they knew so well as they had heard Sabbath to Sabbath of the

Law and the prophets had come to life with excitement and passion when the Man not just recounted and retold them but almost performed the drama of salvation before their very eyes. So caught up were they in the words spinning in a web of revelation of the mysterious ways of Yahweh, they could not hear the sound, interlaced with the verses of the Torah,

Be Not Afraid!

The Stranger spoke with clarity and authority, describing how the Messiah must suffer as Isaiah proclaimed, recounting: "Was it not necessary that the Messiah should suffer these things so as to enter into His glory," these words, they knew from the Scriptures and the scrolls they had unrolled to read, to pray, and to study so often. These words they knew by heart, but today as the Man, all in white, began to espouse these familiar lines, they sounded different, and each sojourner yet to become a pilgrim grew attentive and aware of each word that had a new and vibrant meaning.

They walked; they listened, the words potent and filled with life, for when spoken, they literally were alive. Their hearts, once heavy and filled with grief, were easy and light. The sadness was not gone, but there was a sense of healing calm. Such a feeling of calm with that pervading fragrance, so virtual and real, that it embraced both men with an elixir of cooling balm. Their Friend, Lord and Master was gone, and yet in the midst of sorrow and grief so binding, a Stranger had unleashed a freedom of healing giving them peace. At this point Rufus thought he heard another voice speaking words he thought he was hearing,

Be Not Afraid!

Words, sacred and profound, enlightened their darkened minds and grief-laced hearts. The scent pursuing them since they left Jerusalem and this Stranger appeared, became a perfume, abundant and cascading around them. The darkness, so oppressive before giving way to sunlight and a blue sky, and so different from the darkness and shadows that had erupted on Friday when the Lord bowed His head and died.

Each time Cleopas sought the contours and details of the Stranger's face, the sun blurred his vision so he could not fully perceive the form walking beside him. Shielding his eyes from the light, he thought were just the usual rays and glare of the sun, he failed to sense the physical characteristics of the Man who walked and talked beside him and his companion.

As they continued as a sacred trio to the village of Emmaus, neither man enquired of their Companion of His Name, but instead were in rapt attention as he walked and spoke. With ease and eloquence of style, he quoted line and verse of the Sacred Scriptures without the need to open a scroll. The words had almost a fragrance as they were spoken, surrounding the men on their journey. What began as a hasty retreat from the city of Jerusalem under cover of the fading night had become a pilgrimage, touching their hearts, stirring their minds, and slowing the pace so that they might hear the words spoken by this companion, filling Cleopas and Rufus' befuddled minds with a knowledge of graced insight to turn anxiety to a much cherished peace and calm.

Both men, trained by a rabbi of great repute, understood the passages, but on this journey that began in flight and fright, was paced now by the gait of the Stranger, who had somehow allowed this rash retreat to slow and become a pilgrimage of faith and hope renewed. Minds, once clouded and confused, were open and attentive to the Stranger, whose words began to undermine this unease and disquiet with language of peace and hope that clarified with deeper insights. Such revelation and knowledge was like that of a soothing balm settling their troubled hearts by offering calm in the midst of a belligerent storm. In spite of this newfound understanding, they still had not yet heard the Voice, speaking in clear volume and tone,

Be Not Afraid!

Such calming words of a Stranger, who had become a guide to the inner Mystery of God and the wonders of the Sacred Texts, now mingled with the sweet fragrance of a refreshing odor, and the light that surrounded these men expunged any element of fear or anxiety as time seemed to stand still and disappear and travel proceeded unimpeded by any hint of anxiety, but replaced by new sight and discovery. The men, unaware they had traveled so far in this genuine journey of the heart, had halted, as both sojourners understood they had arrived at the door to their home in Emmaus.

The Stranger continued to proceed in earnest down the same road, as his companions pleaded, "Stay with us for it is nearly evening." The Stranger agreed to accept the hospitality, entering the humble abode that was saturated with an overwhelming fragrance and a burst of light. These men, who had begun this journey in doubt, were renewed in spirit and mind and about to be transformed as the Stranger entered this dwelling and made all that he beheld not just a dwelling but also a home.

Their vision, still clouded, but their minds were afire. At the table, a Stranger no longer, but now a Friend that unknown to each of these men who were followers and disciples, they were about to be transfigured and transformed to witness and become evangelists to see and proclaim the Good News.

Cloaks were hung for they were home. Water was offered to quench their thirst, first for the Stranger and then for the dwellers to wipe away the dust of the road. As they prepared a meal, simple in fare for themselves and their special guest, both men were aware that the scent that journeyed with them embraced the walls of this humble abode.

The Stranger, whose name they did not know, was invited to sit at the table that was set with a meager meal. With simple bread and a jug of average wine, the trio finally rested from the fatigue of the day and the trauma of the days just past. The Stranger was all aglow, in spite of the fading sunlight and the birth of the dawning night. In his hands he held the bread, and in reverence their eyes were fixed on the Stranger's raised hands, holding the bread. He broke the bread, and in that moment of emotional release and discovery of astounding belief, their eyes opened to the new and awesome insight: They saw; they knew; they were free; and the Stranger was recognized as they proclaimed, "It is the Lord," and he was gone. In unison, words, and gestures, they exclaimed, "Were not our hearts burning within us as he spoke!"

Grasping cloaks drenched in the aroma of newfound life and love, they raced breathlessly back to the city just fled, as no longer in fear they heard clearly the words,

Be Not Afraid!

To the upper room, breathlessly they arrived, exclaiming in words and shouts of joy, all mingled together, and proclaiming, "We have seen the Lord, and we are not afraid!"

Chapter Seven: A Centurion Proclaims

For a second night the nightmare had plagued his sleep. Restless and uneasy, Claudius, a centurion in the region of Judea under the authority of Pontius Pilate, the governor, was doomed to sleeplessness these last few nights because of the terror of his actions and what he had witnessed. It was his responsibility to maintain order in the city of Jerusalem and on occasion to execute those condemned by order of Rome. Such executions were quite often and routine except for the One they called Rabbi, and some even claimed he was a Messiah and a King. Claudius knew that this Rabbi's execution was anything but a routine execution. It was filled with drama, intrigue, and even hints of mystery. Who was this Man he had led to that hill called Calvary to die such an ignoble and barbaric death. As the Man hung upon that tree, Claudius, the centurion normally would not give the criminal any attention, but he did glance and almost spied upon this condemned Man. The Man was indeed no common criminal, and as he hung upon that tree in excruciating pain and disgrace he did so with profound dignity.

Never before in all his many years upon the field of battle or enforcement of the Roman law had Claudius seen such a Man. His very face and demeanor indicated no fear. How many had begged for mercy and to be spared but this One offered his hands and arms to the executioners who with deft precision raised the hammer to place the nail to crush bone and tear flesh. The Man raised no protest in a plea to be spared. Waking in his bed during a night of disturbed sleep, Claudius became aware of a scent, powerful yet sweet. Accustomed often to the putrid smells of unwashed bodies, particularly those of his soldiers who perspired profusely under the glare of the unforgiving Judean sun, clothed as they were in garments of metal and bronze. This fragrance was not that of sweat but a unique fragrance that possessed a hint of cleanliness, so foreign to his sense of smell.

Claudius, although lacking sleep was conscious enough to remember that the scent he was inhaling was not obscure from his recent memory. His mind remembered when he had first inhaled such a scent. It was the very day that he was assigned to lead the Rabbi to the hill to be crucified. When Claudius entered the Praetorium, his eyes rested upon the sight of the Man, bloodied and brutally beaten, but standing painfully erect with an air of regal authority.

It was incomprehensible how a Man marked as a criminal and the depiction of that image could disturb the composure of the rugged and hardened Roman soldier. But, it was the Man's eyes and their magnetic gaze that, though swollen and bloodied, cast an aura that bound the centurion by an invisible trance, capturing the one responsible for the prisoner. It was difficult to imagine who was the prisoner and the one bound, for the centurion felt pulled by an unseen thread, connected to the One he must lead to that tree. In that momentary gaze that felt so intense, he was so preoccupied he could not hear a phrase wafted along on the air,

Be Not Afraid!

Then, the Man, stripped and bound to a pillar in the center of the courtyard, awaited the centurion's command to assault and disfigure the prisoner. As by rote and less by authority, Claudius disdained brutality inflicted for sheer game, and raising his hand without voicing the order, unleashed permission for two soldiers, filled with glee, to bestow upon the Man a parting gift from the cruel mind of Pilate and use their straps of leather and metal to riddle the body with marks of devious cruelty and brutal delight. As the source of pain found their mark in bruising, exposing, and tearing the flesh of a gentle Man, and leaving crevices of deep wounds that filled his physical frame with rivulets of blood. It was when the flesh was broken and the blood ran bold, that the centurion became aware of the scent that caressed his senses while the soldiers under his command were torturing the Man, now bound and held. Not only were his senses taken in by the sight of the Man, but in his smell, he inhaled a heavenly perfume defying the sight of hellish and gruesome thrills. The centurion's senses were under siege, for his hearing was as impaired as his sight was distracted. Even so, he could slightly hear that phrase repeated in clear articulate words, speaking to assure,

Be Not Afraid!

He glanced quickly all around to find who had spoken, and his eyes met those of the Rabbi that were filled with such pain but in spite of his agony, Claudius sensed such a nobility of character that he had to look away, and yet he heard again, even louder, almost as if in command,

Be Not Afraid!

The Prisoner, now spent with blood and gore, was released from the bondage of his chains and freed from scourging. But devious wits would not be satisfied with the amount of blood that had been paid in tribute to evil but demanded more coins in retribution and so devised more brutality to inflict on the beaten Man. With a display of newfound savagery they mocked and berated him with sneering looks and vicious, obscene words as they called him a king. With purple cloth stolen from a horse's back to serve as a regal robe they draped it around his shoulders in ridicule of royalty and kingship, and for a crown of cruel hoax, instead of gems they used thorns that do not adorn but injure and bruise to place on the Man's head.

It was such a ghastly sight that others turned quickly away in fear and to shed a tear. The centurion was used to savagery and the games of abuse inflicted upon the innocent and the guilty alike because they were simply bored and mean; however, this day he was grieved by such an undiluted display of violence. The Man, broken in body but not spirit, was in great pain but he raised his face, bleeding and disfigured as it was, to seek out the face of the centurion, and as their eyes met interlocked in grief, he was so sure he heard coming from the Man the words,

Be Not Afraid!

In this theater of cruelty and pain, Claudius called the men to attention to escort the prisoner to the seat of judgment and to await the verdict that would be proclaimed by the man who held the reins of life and death, Pontius Pilate. This was neither a dream nor a nightmare that had gone awry as Claudius remembered it, as he pulled himself from his bed, disturbed by the sights that continued to race through his mind. He noticed again the scent pervading his quarters, separate from the soldiers' barracks, and though still night; a glow surrounded the space, not a glow from the use of oil, but a glow from another source of radiant light. Almost as if a Voice had spoken, Claudius turned to see who had uttered those words he had heard in the haze of dreams but now heard so clear, detailed and real in his awakened state . . .

Be Not Afraid!

He looked, but no one was present even though he did hear and recall that dreadful day just two days past when he was so afraid, a fear not of battle but of a spiritual force that enclosed the Rabbi on the Cross. The dignity he showed in contrast to the pain inflicted. The compassion he had shown to others as he was now jeered and abused along the Way. These struck Claudius with a degree of insight that this was no ordinary Man to surpass the regal dignity he observed throughout this horrid ordeal. Somehow the centurion grasped something so extraordinary that he dared to admit that he saw Divinity displayed.

With heaviness of heart, he had followed the command and had led the Man to the hill. How odd, he thought, that as the centurion, he was in command, but not on this day as he fought against the climb to that hill and the penalty he was called to execute, for the Man had willingly taken the Cross and the pain and with each excruciating footstep had led the way to that hill. With hammer and nail, the Man's body was contorted and splayed upon the wood when the gibbet was reached and raised between the atmosphere of heaven and earth.

For three hours amidst the searing pain, the dying criminal, who was called the Rabbi and hailed a Messiah and King, proclaimed a litany of mercy and a message of forgiveness and love from the Cross, which was his pulpit. As his head bowed and his soul escaped, the earth rocked and quaked as the heavens wept, for the Man now dead was nothing less, as the centurion had witnessed and proclaimed in his own voice, "Truly, this Man was the Son of God."

Such a profession of faith by the centurion made him a prisoner these last two days, in agony over the drama that he had witnessed unfold. As morning broke on this third day since the event, light and a scent burst into the room as the fragrance embraced his solid frame, and he noticed a form move closer and say ...

Be Not Afraid!

The centurion knelt before the dazzling apparition he recognized and proclaimed "My Lord" on this third day. He was no longer afraid, as the Man, bright and filled with light, raised the centurion from his knees to bathe him in grace, and he heard distinctly and clearly the words that bring him tears of joy . . .

Be Not Afraid!

Chapter Eight: Homecoming at Bethany

The three could not sleep. Even Martha, often so busy with many things, was unusually quiet and inactive. The kitchen, normally a beehive of activity with preparations of meals in getting ready for guests, was deserted. Around the table were the unwashed dishes left in haste and unattended. No one was hungry or even cared to eat. The last three days had been days of horror, pain, and suffering for the Master. The One they so loved had been taken from them and killed upon a tree. Martha's face was scarred by the ravishments of grief for she had lost a cherished and dear friend. But Martha knew Jesus was more than that, for Jesus was Lord. She recalled in sadness the death of Jesus upon the Cross, when her little, safe and secure world of Bethany shattered and was torn asunder during the midday storm and earthquake that shook Jerusalem, but it seemed that all the world had convulsed that day her Lord was killed. Her sadness was unlike that over the loss of her brother, Lazarus, who after a serious but brief illness succumbed to the grasp of the tomb, only to be freed by the Master's voice telling her brother to come forth. Who, Martha wondered, would call the Master forth from the tomb that now held him captive in the tight and unrelenting grip of death for these three days.

She yearned to hear the Master's voice just once again, but all she heard was the heavy breath of silence speaking of death. How she wished to see the Master sitting in her home on a cushion as he spoke to all in the crowded room. But there was no cushion, only the hard stone upon which the Master's body had been laid, not to rest but in death to mock humanity and all who prayed in hope of the triumph of life. There were no crowds this day, for the crowds had vanished when the Master bowed his head and died upon that tree. They had fled to their homes, for death was the victor they had thought, and they had despaired for with the Master dead, hope had withered and blown away in the storm, destroying all remnants of joy and leaving only the debris of fear in its place.

Except for her sister, Mary, and her brother, Lazarus, the house and the rooms were eerily empty and quiet. At the rear in a separate room was Mary, the Mother of Jesus, who had come to stay with them for Passover. It was to be a celebration, but began to unfold as a tragedy of unparalleled dimensions when word came to Bethany that Jesus had been betrayed and was a captive of the High Priest and the Romans. After the Friday of grief and death, and a hasty burial, the Mother was brought to the house that Jesus so loved so that she might mourn the loss of the Son she so loved, while others were crying for the hope that had been slain on the Cross and was now gone.

How could this be? The Master who could raise Lazarus from the grave, calm the sea, feed thousands with a few loaves of bread and some fish, and amaze vast crowds with his words and parables, was silent, bound by a shroud and held captive by a stone. Martha's mind raced over the events of the last days that had passed, and suddenly she sniffed a fragrance of startling compound and texture, and she realized the scent was the same as that of the ointment poured over the feet of her Lord, just days before his death upon the Cross. At that moment, the Mother of Jesus appeared before her and in knowledge of a spirituality that defied reason embraced her friend and exclaimed . . .

Be Not Afraid!

The house was illuminated by a torrent of light that wrapped the Mother, Martha, Mary, and Lazarus in a clothing of grace. The air was saturated with the aroma of love, and the four embraced and declared in one voice, "We have seen the Lord." Mary raced towards the source of such brilliance, and as she came close to it, she swooned and fell to her knees. Lazarus, in fleeing death's grip, absorbed this moment of life and expressed in words uttered in deep faith and delight, "My Lord!" Once bound in the tomb himself and set free by the Man, standing before him, Lazarus understood more deeply than the others experiencing the restoration of the breath of life to a decaying form. Released from the tomb, he stood before his Lord, who was not newly restored but resurrected, never to die again. Lazarus sensed a new order striking at the heart of the reign of sin. Regained, restored, Paradise renewed, and exploding in cascading light to embrace the house.

The light saturated all within the space, as Martha, spellbound by the medicine of grace, savored the light, luxuriating in the moment and inhaling the exotic fragrance that beat with the reborn rhythm of life. The Mother and the friends were breathing a crisp air that enclosed the room and made them all swoon.

In the midst of this swirl of air, light and fragrance, as their senses were touched by another world's embrace, they knew in their own hearts and surely sensed that the Presence they felt was the One they were mourning. But, as if by some mystery they could not fully absorb, they spoke out in the language of love and said what they think: "How can this be?" and sounds, wrapped in an emotional tide, rushed over them . . .

Be Not Afraid!

A Mother who once had conversed with heavenly hosts and with friends had entertained the One so many in this land had called Lord, had witnessed the stone of death crushed by the Rabbi, who claimed to be the Son of God, and had returned to life a brother, freed from the grasp of death. From unbelief to reverent praise, the sisters experienced the power of grace and love, bursting the chains of death, forged by the powers of Hell, and had given breath to a brother and dear friend to return to the land of the living one who was dead and was now living and free. How was it, they wondered over these three days could the Lord raise another through the sound of his voice but still be bound by the prison of death. Grief and sorrow mingled this day after Sabbath morn with an abundance of light seizing the house, and the air, perfumed with an extraordinary scent.

The Mother, all aglow, knew what Martha, Mary and Lazarus were about to discover. In the midst of grief and a covering of sorrow, they pondered the events as they had unfolded. Just days before these awful sights were branded into their living memory; cross and nails, the brutal scourging, the unjust sentencing and illegal trials, the screams of the frenzied mob shouting, "Crucify him, crucify him," the three faithful friends had seen Jesus killed and buried. They mourned this loss but remained perplexed and confused because in their midst was Lazarus, a brother once dead now living and breathing because of the Master. They wondered without speaking why such power was not being used to lift the veil of death and set the Rabbi free! But no answer availed; only a whisper, exhaling and offering comfort as they heard expressed a virtual embrace, depicted as breeze and sound . . .

Be Not Afraid!

The light enclosed all in the house, and the Mother, joining them, exclaimed for all to hear, "He is here!" The fragrance was overpowering, and Lazarus remembered the smell when he was summoned from the grave, released from the tomb, and brought back to life. They swooned under the weight of grace and light and were dazed by the overpowering odor of life. The fragrance and light mingled and blended, uniting in form and breath. The mist of unbelief and dismay dissipated, and the fog of memory rose, and the sight appeared. The Mother exclaimed in a joyous refrain as the Light became a shape and Lazarus, Mary and Martha proclaimed, "It is the Lord," and they knelt. The Man in full stature was more than just a form but by all appearance the One they recognized and clearly saw and heard as he said . . .

Be Not Afraid!

Time stood still, as they gazed in adoration. The minutes moved slowly. Incredible, astounding, remarkable were the simple words they used to define this supernatural sight. No language, no art or words could describe or impress upon their reason what was totally unreasonable and quite illogical. Human standards could not be applied. Reason had limits and could not fathom the depth of Divinity nor scan the width of the mercy of God.

The arms, wounded and so scarred, were raised in a benediction and blessing as this scene of the tableau of faith unfolded: The Mother, transfixed for the Annunciation and the greeting of Gabriel, coming full circle to gather her strength and embrace the Son; the Son yielding to the touch of the earth and allowing the Mother to breach the divide between life and death; around her, the trio of the sisters and brother absorbing this fount of splendor cascading before them in magnificent wonder. Then in a flash all at once, the same Voice hummed through the room and the house . . .

Be Not Afraid!

The sister of Lazarus, Mary by name who sat at the feet of Jesus, would never be the same. Dancing and singing to the praise and glory of God the Most High, she knew that God indeed had done wonderful things. The house filled with delight as these companions of the One they called Son and Lord had visited his people and set them free.

Lazarus, though alive and well, prayed for the grace to go where his Master lived on. He grieved no longer for the body in the grave, but mourned that he could not go where the Risen One had paved a new road for others to escape a life of sin and death and revel in the light and life of grace that was everywhere this day, but so few realized all had been saved.

Martha, busy with so many things, wished to rest and enter the haze where memory and grace united to offer a trembling heart the space to enjoy the touch of the Lord, who had visited them from on high to sanctify them in healing and hope.

Finally, the Mother, looking at all three, repeated in joy the phrase, known by all so well . . .

Be Not Afraid!

Chapter Nine: Nicodemus and Joseph of Arimathea

He could not sleep. The ghastly images invaded his twilight period between rest and waking moments. The grotesque depictions of the Man stretched out upon the bloodstained wood tortured his dreams and turned them into nightmares. The Rabbi was dead, and the Pharisee, Nicodemus, a good and upright man, felt more than just the effects of a sleepless night. It was not the lack of sleep but the full weight of a troubled conscience and a heavy heart that disturbed his sleep.

For Nicodemus, the Rabbi called Jesus had been more than a political problem but a mysterious and supernatural question that the Torah and the theological debates of scholars and teachers of the Law could not fully comprehend. In the days before the celebration of Passover, the city of Jerusalem had been embroiled in the semantics of political and theological intrigue as this Jesus captivated the hearts of the people.

Not just the common people, not just the poor and the outcast, but the leaders of the Sanhedrin who had been paying close attention to Jesus. Some like Nicodemus were more than just fascinated with him; they secretly began to hope and desire that this Man was the Messiah, the One that the people of Israel were waiting to come and save them. The poor, the outcast, the sinner, and even the leaders of the people were drawn to Jesus, and Nicodemus was like so many whose hearts hoped that Jesus was the One.

The people opened not just their hearts to Jesus, but one Sunday morning they had opened the city's gates and covered the streets with cloaks, as the Man astride a donkey was hailed as Messiah and King. They waved palm branches as their voices sang, "Hosanna!" From the heights of Fort Antonia and the Temple compound, soldiers and priests in masked fear and hidden anxiety had glared down upon the unfolding scene. The clamor of so many mingled voices had prevented any from hearing the whispered voice echoing around them . . .,

Be Not Afraid!

Nicodemus was afraid. He had been so since the day three years before when John the Baptist attested to and confirmed that Jesus was the One that Israel had been waiting for. Three years of ministry that had seen massive crowds awaiting his words, he had become amazed and captivated by his miracles and astonished by his compassion and passion for others.

The well-ordered world of Nicodemus, grounded in the constancy of Yahweh and the certainty of the Torah, had been shattered as Nicodemus gravitated to this Man and was charmed by his words. When he heard Jesus speak, the Torah sprang to life. When Jesus healed the sick and made the blind see, the deaf hear, and the lame walk again, Nicodemus felt the sure presence of the compassion of God in the midst of everyday life, and, if he listened carefully, he could feel and hear the whisper that became a Voice . . .

Be Not Afraid!

Nicodemus might have heard the words, but he was afraid. He had been trapped by a fear of what others might think or judge him by since he had been pleased to be with the Man from Galilee. He had played it safe, and under the cover and protection of night sought the wisdom of the One they now mourned. He was confused and frightened no longer. Courage once benign had exploded in grief and devotion. When the pall of death covered the face of the Rabbi called Jesus from Nazareth on that dreadful day, he proclaimed to the governor his request to bury the Man now dead and to do so with dignity and respect. Nicodemus, unchained from the bonds of fear, clearly heard the whispered Voice . . .

Be Not Afraid!

And with courage magnified, he had claimed the body of the Man hanging dead upon the Cross.

The sleepless nights since that stark burial had disturbed his nights and days with unsettled thoughts of regret and inner agony. "Truly, truly, I say unto you, unless one is born of water and the Spirit, he cannot enter into the Kingdom of God. That which is born of the flesh is flesh, and that which is born of the Spirit is spirit . . ." And the words drifted into the inner space of his mind and heart over and over again. A wise man of many matters, he could not comprehend that such Divine Truth, born of another realm, a world so distant from the one they were living in here and now. Seated in a cushioned chair beside the bed he had not ruffled these three days, he was awake while the Man he had grown to know and love lay still in the grave.

Broken down and weeping, Nicodemus had lost, not just a cherished friend, but a wisdom-filled guide and mentor. This Companion had cast the world in a new vision of splendor in an array of colors of grace, but now he was filled with a dark despair, as he wept and heard again words so loud and clear . . .

Be Not Afraid!

He turned to see who was speaking and was engulfed by an awesome Light and his senses were enflamed by a fragrance of love and pure delight. As the mist of the glaring Light dissipated, he saw, he believed and he fully understood, for no longer was he afraid.

Meanwhile, the man called Joseph from Arimathea, another captured by the fragrance and the Light, returned to the spot where he had buried his Lord. He approached the tomb through a garden in full bloom. Puzzled, he stared, for the stone was askew and rolled off its base. The opening to the grave was filled with a spontaneous burst of Light and a fragrance, unfamiliar but of great delight and warm and pleasant comfort. Joseph savored these sensory experiences and wondered what they might be as he was feeling both joy and sorrow.

Cautiously, he approached the open and abandoned grave, and as he did so he heard a Voice he knew so well proclaim loud and clear . . .

Be Not Afraid!

His heart racing, he was embraced by a holy light and a heavenly sight, and no longer did he walk in the darkness, but moved towards the aperture of the tomb, all aglow. Arms outstretched, he tried to grasp the vision he beheld, and he believed the impossible. Instead of his heart, it was his feet that raced from the tomb that no longer held death. He returned to the city, yet asleep, to the home of Nicodemus, fully awake not from sleep but from the grip of fear. As the men encountered one another, they embraced, no longer sharing their grief but in the incredible knowledge that God was so near!

In excitement and the wonder of disbelief, the men, one a Pharisee and the other a man of wealth and status, exclaimed in a tumble of words, set free and unbound, that the Rabbi was alive! Part of a devoted but silent group of disciples, the men had been distraught by the death of this Man. They knew he had offered hope to Israel and the lands beyond. In the darkness and cruelty of the crucifixion they had witnessed, they requested from Pilate the Body of the One, sinless but so disfigured. In grief, they transported the body of their Lord to the tomb of Joseph. Picture this scene of tenderness and love as Nicodemus with outstretched arms carried one hundred pounds of aromatic essence and anointed and bathed the body of the One they called the Messiah.

The fragrance that once covered the dead seeped into the room, and Joseph and Nicodemus in adulation and joy twirled for they had seen the Lord. He entered the abode, and the men sang, "Hosanna, laud to the King!" In the excitement of the moment, overwhelmed by the light and the fragrance, they smiled with abandon and heard his Voice, so strong and so near, and they knew truly it was he, as they felt its power and warmth...

Be Not Afraid!

Puzzled by the apparition for the men had observed the Mission from a distance, they were humbled by such attention and bent their knees before the Presence of the Light and

Fragrance that assaulted and then lovingly embraced them. Swooning with exuberance and exhilaration, these men of reason wondered if their minds were faltering and falling asunder of reality and truth.

Hearts racing, they felt the inexpressible beauty surrounding them, for no dogma had yet to attest that from death could rise life. Death had been conquered, and the grave was no longer the holder of grief. Heaven this day was married to the glory of creation and displayed to Nicodemus and Joseph the gracious love of a tender Deity, uttering in life, light and scent . . .

Be Not Afraid!

From this message in spirit and flesh, Nicodemus and Joseph, no longer in the shadows but now in full sunlight, proclaimed in words of courage and witness "This was no ordinary man but One who saves, just risen from the grave. No stone can hold the glory; no shroud contain Divinity; and no darkness can hide the abundance of pure Light." Two men, once grieving, now believed, and in the drama of a new language of faith were inclined to see when before they were blind; and with renewed and refined senses, they heard, whereas in the past they were deaf; and no longer mute, they proclaimed with energy and vigor of the newfound life that the Master once dead was fully alive! In strong and rising voices, these two, once skeptics, became believers and affirmed disciples. Reborn with the beauty of a baptism of breath restored, they heard clearly, distinctly, and profoundly these words, as if they were a newborn's cries . . .

Be Not Afraid!

Chapter Ten: By the Sea of Tiberius; Peter

The water always offered him a sense of certainty, peace, and comfort. In these days of anguish and disturbance, he craved such a source of solace while in the midst of powerful and dramatic emotions. Such emotions rushed into his mind like an avalanche, stirring his soul to a boiling point and causing his soul to hunger to a point of spiritual starvation. He was dealing with the aftermath of the past few days and nights that had been habitually dark and gloomy no matter the time of day. Emotions that scarred and seared his soul to haunt his mind were not easily dissolved in the waters of a turbulent climate of uncertainty and anxiety.

How could the impossible become possible? The astounding events of that week were indelibly etched into his memory. How could he betray the One who had called him, a mere man named Simon, to come and follow? Follow, Simon had. In a moment, he had abandoned boat and nets to see where the Rabbi would lead on a journey of faith. Such a journey had included a mystery yet to be revealed in words to be spoken and heard, in visions of a Kingdom, not of this world, and in teachings with authority that amazed and terrified any who listened. Who was this Man who turned water into wine, walked upon water unfettered, healed the lame so they might walk again, made the blind see and awaken to new sights and wonders, gave the mute newfound voices so they might sing and delight the Lord in song, and opened the ears of the deaf to the sounds of life, for the Spirit was upon this unique and special Man, who had summoned the fisherman to walk alongside him.

Now twisted in mind and heart, he felt so withered for the words spoken that night just a few days earlier tormented his life. Why could he not have just listened to the Master at that Last Supper, when he had said that Simon the fisherman would betray him in word and deed, and yet he was filled with pride and would not believe. Blinded not by sight but with bluster and bravado, he was captive to pride, causing him to deny the One who had called him to follow him, that day along the shore and he had. This same Man with accuracy would predict the truth that a rooster's crow would mark his fall, so hard a fall that he could not hear the Voice, speaking with love and care . . .

Be Not Afraid!

The words, "I do not know that Man," still screamed within his own hearing, and the voice that was his and his alone that had uttered such a testimony of cosmic betrayal, tortured his soul and caused his dreams to venture into the realm of nightmares.

The words, the look, the embarrassment, and the shock. The big fisherman had voiced the words that were abhorrent and as painful as the kiss the traitor had dared give the Master on the cheek. The Master had turned to look at him as the rooster gave the verdict, but the Master's gaze was not in disdain but in mercy. Fleeing the courtyard and the volley of tears that were his just sentence, he carried the heavy and awful burden and would continue to do so for years. To the tomb, he had raced that Sunday when the news had reached the Upper Room, but he found only an empty, bare tomb. The tomb however, was no longer cold with the sting of death but warmed with the joy of hope and the birth of new life.

On that first evening of confusion and doubt through barred doors and hearts, the Master had appeared full of Light, so white and clear, and yet in a disturbance of nature embroiling them all. He was not dead but appeared before them to speak words so all could hear . . .

Be Not Afraid!

The days that followed had nursed his soul to newfound health and had healed the heaviness he held deep within. He could not forget those words spoken in fear and in such haste. He could not undo what had been said and with each apparition of his Lord and Savior, the one known as Simon bowed his head and implored his Lord to forgive such a transgression that a proud heart had exploded as venom to harm the Lord. Each look caused not inner healing but a continued agony of sorrow and contrition not fully accorded. In turmoil, the fisherman could not hear the words of assurance his Lord was proclaiming . . .

Be Not Afraid!

On this day so many since the Lord first had appeared, Simon's heart was still heavy, so he took to the sea, seeking comfort and peace that the waters so often offered. The sun this morning caressed him. The task and work of fishing invigorated him. In the boat were his partner and friend, Andrew, his brother. His familiar face offered Simon a sense of firmness in an evaporating world. They fished, they caught, they mended nets, all under the gaze of heaven, and a radiant blue sky, and the Master appeared out of nowhere, on the shore. Andrew was the first to notice the Rabbi, who walked along the shore, and how strange, for three years ago he was the first to see him, and today in this time of miracles he again noticed the figure on shore and instinctively knew it was the Lord! So it was the brother, Andrew, who informed Simon that before him was the Lord. Without hesitation or wondering, but with firm resolve and assured faith, he looked, saw, and recognized the One who is Lord. Jumping into the sea, half-naked and without regard for security or safety, he swam frantically to shore so that he might embrace his Lord. With the boat in tow, Simon and Andrew came together upon the beach and awkwardly fumbled to cover themselves in their meager attire so that they could meet and greet the One who was waiting for them.

All around, they felt a gentle breeze, and in that breeze a Voice, strong and sure, confident and pleasing, and the brothers heard in the whisper of clarity and love . . .

Be Not Afraid!

A brazier of charcoal, all aglow, the Man in stunning and immaculate white had prepared a meal. The Man knew that those who had come ashore were hungry, but hungry for more than plain food. They were seeking a morsel of surety and proof of some reality that death had been burst asunder and was no longer victor but vanquished. The Man, standing in a brilliant array of a white color that no earthly bleach could foster and whose face was shinning bright with a gleaming smile and tender features had greeted the fishermen with a soothing Voice. With a calm and measured beat, he said, "Peace be to you," and offered them bread and fish to eat. They accepted the invitation with gracious dignity, for the moment was no ordinary incident but a remarkable display of divine joviality. The fishermen, accustomed to the hazards of the seas, had stood upon the land in amazement, for the land beneath their feet had felt shaky as they had comprehended the implausible.

Each appearance of the Man, arrayed in such Light held fascination and delight for all who witnessed each moment of supernatural sight. Unknown to those who sat, ate and simply stared for the Man returned the look with ample insight that made the fisherman uneasy as he bowed his head low to avoid the glare and trembled to hear the Voice he knew so well.

Simon, hearing, raised his head to look at the Man who was standing and gazing intensely at the fisherman. "Son of John, do you love me?" he said. The question asked, the fisherman heard and in a stuttering tone answered, "Yes, Lord, you know that I love you." The Man in white, with a look to penetrate Simon's heart, said to the man who had betrayed him, "Feed my lambs." Silence followed, as the words filtered into the sinews of his body and bones. At first, they seemed an embrace, strong and loving, but then he heard again, "Simon, son of John, do you love me?" He wondered. Did he not hear my first response? But clearly and with ardent zeal, he responded, "Yes, Lord, you know that I love you." The big fisherman sighed as the words were released, like a calming salve to soothe an aching heart. Tears welled up from within and began to tumble down the face of the fisherman as the Man said, "Tend my sheep." The eyes of the man, Simon, and the Lord were locked in a gaze. Andrew realized he was witnessing a delicate moment, more than ordinary but potent with the saliva of grace and the breath of mercy.

Andrew could not look away and felt the tears well up, finding himself a companion to his brother in weeping as he sensed the import of this remarkable encounter of confession and repentance. Again, the Man, still staring and gazing, asked the question, leaving the hearer distressed and disturbed. "Simon, son of John, do you love me?" Almost as if choking back a volley of tears, Simon meekly uttered, "Lord, you know everything. You know that I love you." No rooster but the sun in full bloom rained down shards of dazzling light, and Simon knew full well the thrice-asked question was healing the three denials, and the heart was made whole.

In a flash, the Man was gone, and the brothers were the only company they saw. But before they left, they heard that Voice, assuring and pleasing ...

Be Not Afraid!

Chapter Eleven: In the Aftermath: John

The days since the dramatic events upon that hill of Golgotha had been days of fear and despair for the apostle of the Master. He had buried the Master after seeing him suffer so upon that wood of the Cross and ultimately die. In a borrowed tomb, he had laid him and watched, as they hastily had sealed the tomb because evening was coming, and the Sabbath had called for rest.

But, there was no Sabbath rest for those who had witnessed the cruel and ignominious death of the gentle Rabbi many had called the Messiah. John was the youngest of the sacred clan of apostles that had followed the Master, since he and his brother had been called to leave their boat and nets to follow him. For three years, he and his brother, along with the other ten, had followed this Man from one town to the next, proclaiming a message of peace and hope and calling people to repent and believe. And believe he did in this Man of wisdom, faith, and mysterious powers. John had seen this Rabbi preach to thousands, heal the crippled, forgive the sinner, and confront the forces of sin and oppression. This day, the third since the awful horror he had witnessed as his Master and Lord was hanged in agony upon that tree of sorrow and pain, was trying to recall when he had witnessed another event, not too long ago. He, Peter and James had journeyed with Jesus to the top of Mount Tabor, and in a blast of supernatural fervor, they had witnessed this simple Rabbi arrayed in glory and majesty. Today, however, as hard as he tried to imagine that scene of transfiguration and glory, John could not hide from the reality he was facing. The

One who could appear in such radiant glory was dead and buried in a tomb, his body, disfigured and possessing no hint of that glory. No breath of living pulsed through his frame, clothed not in supernatural light but instead wrapped tight in a shroud that could not hide the wounds nor prevent the blood from seeping into the cloth and soiling the fabric, holding the Man a prisoner of death. But what John would recall and remember was that despite the coldness of the tomb, the depth of grief, and the sorrow overwhelming them all, a pleasing fragrance saturated the rough-hewn environment with a pleasing odor to bless those assembled for such a despairing act of burying a Man, so young but loved so well. As they rolled the stone, grating against the rock and soil, to close the opening of the tomb, John and the others could not hear the Voice calling after them . . .

Be Not Afraid!

At the Cross, he had stood with the Mother of the Man, hanged so painfully upon the wood. At first, he had run with the others, afraid of becoming a victim and facing the same ordeal as his Lord. How shamed he had felt when all scattered, just as the Master had foretold. But grace and courage had returned that night, and with steely resolve he had journeyed to the house of Caiaphas with Simon the fisherman to see what would transpire during this night of mystery, grace, and fright. Arriving, they discovered that the house was aflame with the passion of discourse and agitation. In the midst, the Man had been bound and silent before the forces of deceit and confusion. They had watched, they had listened, and they had prayed. In the jumble of accusations, John was distracted and did not see the exchange between Simon and the maid who had accused him of being a follower of the Man who was bound and before the Sanhedrin. Before the cock crowed, the Lord, embroiled in history and Truth, was denied not once but thrice, and the fisherman who had been told beforehand but did not believe, left in tears, distraught that he had denied the One he claimed was Lord and had fallen into treachery. He raced out, as John had not comprehended until he heard the rooster crow, and the fisherman was gone in a flash, and then he recalled the prediction of the Master at the Last Supper. In the confusion and mania that grasped the night with fear abounding in a wave of evil and discord, even John could not hear the Voice, calling out to sooth and reassure,

Be Not Afraid!

In that moment, three days hence, he had been caught in a spasm of convulsing tears, rocking his body and breaking his spirit. He missed the Master. He was sorrowful and filled with pain and regret. He fled but returned and with the Mother, he had journeyed with the Man along that path of sorrow and tears to the Cross. Each step the Master had taken was filled with pain and agony. The Mother had felt each stumble and every degree of pain that the Child she had borne suffered along this way of sorrow. A sword of misery and anguish pierced her heart, shattering it into so many pieces, assailing her composure and her courage. Her faith, however, remained solid and untouched by the savagery of that day, as what she had witnessed was brutal and unrelenting. She recalled the terror that had struck her heart so many years earlier when an aged priest had held the

Child in joy and then gazed upon the Woman, envisioning this day clearly as it had unfolded this very day. In his eyes she had seen the sadness and terror.

The Mother, standing beneath the Cross, for three hours had watched every breath of the Son she so loved and adored, taper in strength, slow, and then move towards death. The young man with her became a force of strength upon whom she now relied. The taunts she had heard, the nails she had seen, the Child she had held so disfigured and suffering. The imaginary sword had plunged into her chest, spoiling the heart forged as one with the Son in agony upon the wood. She had felt the hands holding her tight, and the apostle's strong arms held her firm through the terror as her heart felt each struggling breath and experienced the harshness of the mockery from the people who were her very own. He had held her close as her Son struggled to survive the onslaught of the coming night of darkness and death. He had tried to protect her from what would happen, but she had protested and wished to witness this moment that no Archangel had ever foretold and that the cryptic message of a priest and prophetess had tried to reveal, but she had not understood. Upon that hill, surrounded by a wave of hate and pain, the Son she had said "yes" to so many years ago was about to die the death of a criminal in infamy and failure. But she had believed that even in that moment God would stand true to his promise, and at the foot of that Cross, John thought he heard the Master say in the midst of such confusion . . .

Be Not Afraid!

John thought that he just imagined what he had heard, but the Mother stood tall and firm for she did hear and did believe, and her courage was renewed but her sorrow and grief remained overflowing, drowning her heart so pierced. The words had fallen upon a maddening crowd, intent on hatred and not remorse. "Father, forgive them for they know not what they do!" The crowd had only screamed louder with a vehemence mixed with rage. "Behold, this day you will be with me in Paradise!" A criminal wept, not in regret but in joy, for the One whom they were defiling, had just whispered sweet grace into his ears, and he felt the warmth of love in the midst of a cruel and ugly world. Gazing with love, she had glimpsed through his labored breathing and his face so assaulted with blood and spit, and heard the gargled Voice, "Woman, behold your Son!" And she had wept, for he had cared and loved her to this bitter end. What a faithful Son. In the midst of his suffering, he did the one thing left to do: entrusting the care of his Mother to the one he so loves and trust, and turning to the man, he commanded: "Son, behold your Mother!" As the skies darkened and the wind whirled round the scene, they embraced, this newfound Mother and son, and heard loud and clear . . .

Be Not Afraid!

John wept when he recalled the scene beneath the Cross, as the Mother swooned and fell and he had braced her fall. They heard the words, "I Thirst!" Will no one relieve this suffering and give this Man a drink to quench the desire of Divinity to embrace all humanity in the arms of love, for he yearned that all may be saved, seeking to do more in the moments that hang in the womb of eternity, waiting for the birth of redemption. Then the words that echo down through the ages: "It is finished," and proclaiming in near jubilation, "Father, into your hands I commend my Spirit!" The Son bowed his head and died. The earth quaked and shook. The skies grew dark and menacing. The solid land rocked and convulsed. The city in view rumbled, and the stones burst and crumbled. The skies in a release, both angry and cleansing, poured down rain in a cascade that drowned the mob in the sobering reality that the heavens were weeping. Something so momentous had just transpired that in the blast of thunder and crash of lightning they could not hear the Voice, shouting in jubilation and acclaim . . .

Be Not Afraid!

Only the Mother and newfound son heard because the others were racing in fear to escape the onslaught of nature, furious that God had bowed his head and died because of Love. The image of the Mother and Son was seared into his mind, as John had watched in silence as the Man who would heal and save was laid dead into the grieving Mother's arms. An iconic sight to move the heart in pain and sadness, that a Son so obedient to the will of the Lord would give his life's breath and suffer human death. John might be called the son now, but the tableau he saw unfolding beneath the Cross was meant for the Mother and the Son alone. When the tears had been spent and the shudders of grief subsided, the son, born again within the shadow of the Cross, had offered a hand to the Mother to wind the body in a shroud of death. As he had approached in reverence and silence, he received the gift of the scent, so pleasing and fragrant in the midst of such ugliness and the foul odor of death, and grief had offered a healing balm to ease the sorrow as he had reached to touch the body and prepare the sacred form for the coldness of the tomb. The scent had risen as incense, as John and men of repute and dignity had offered the service of burial, even as they moved in utter disbelief.

Quickly before sunset they must do this deed of charity. Close by was a tomb offered by a friend, and with limited time they wrapped the body in the winding sheet, saturated by the blood of the One who shed his blood first on the table of the Last Supper and completely now upon the wood of the Cross. In the midst of such splendor of theology and grace, the body of the Son bound by death was lifted from the dirt, saturated with the water of the cleansing deluge and the Blood of the Lamb, sacrificed for the human race. The scent of atonement stirred the heart, beating in gratitude for the mystery yet to unfold, but for today and at this time was trapped by death. The march to the tomb was somber and tearful. All the senses were assaulted, and in contradiction and confusion, the heart and ears could not hear the whisper of a loving God saying . . .

Be Not Afraid!

The son, just proclaimed beneath the Cross, was holding the Woman, his mother, as she staggered to the tomb to bury her only Son, made so by the fiat she uttered so long ago. That "yes," proclaimed in its fullest speech, as the Son was laid in death upon the slab of stone. In darkness, they departed to watch in painful sight, as the stone that attested to the departing of life was rolled to the opening to block any light. The finality of the moment bore such weight, for unknowing, they must wait for the rays of the sun to burst the chains of death and free the Man who had journeyed to hell to bring the Good News.

Be Not Afraid!

Now the third day and still consumed with grief, John, the faithful and dear friend, was blinded by the Light, radiating and enveloping him in the glare of grace and blessing. He was overcome by the Light that had entered the room and had mixed with the familiar scent that had touched his senses first at the Cross and then at the tomb. In a rare instance when eternity and time stood still, the man, who was grieving, was now smiling for in the midst of this powerful radiance he sees, he knows, he fully understands. He bowed his head and knelt, hearing so clearly and distinctly as his heart leapt with joy and belief . . .

Be Not Afraid!

Chapter Twelve: The Odd Couple: Pilate and Caiaphas

Both men of power and stature, they were unnerved by the sights and feeling of the unsettled earth as it quaked and swooned, when at midday the heavens were spent, and the Rabbi bowed his head upon the wood and was declared dead. One was a man of power, made secure by the military arm and muscle of Rome, while the other was supposedly a man of prayer and letters who held power, not in arms but in the authority of an unseen God and letters contained within sacred scrolls. Worlds apart by philosophy, culture and faith these men were bound together by an unholy alliance of expediency and need this day. This Rabbi was a revolutionary, not in deed but in thought. Imagine teaching the people to call God, Father, and dare to address the unseen deity as Abba! More than just revolutionary, but these were words that stirred people to disobedience against the authority of their leaders and priests. The Rabbi was himself in contradiction with the teachings of these men of letters and the Torah they feared because what he taught they considered blasphemy, and such they could not tolerate.

Pontius Pilate was amused during the trial to see the High Priest and his Sanhedrin cronies squirming beneath their delicate robes as they attempted to navigate the harsh terrain of subterfuge and deceit under the glare of Rome and the people's eyes. The Man standing before him was not guilty. Pilate knew enough about how power worked and how one preserved such power in the face of such a challenge by the Man from Nazareth.

This Man was not afraid of the High Priest, or any of the Jewish leaders. That was clear when he had upset the Temple moneychangers, much to the chagrin of the Jewish leaders but to the delight of the people who often felt betrayed by the ones chosen to show them the way to Yahweh but often kept the road blocked or too expensive to travel. The gentle Rabbi was showing the people a different way, and they were delighted to listen, follow, and obey. This was more than just a well-loved teacher; this Man in the minds of the High Priest and the leaders, was too dangerous. The people had to be protected from the infectious disease of his renegade teachings. Pilate was brought into this conversation and the actions that this discourse would achieve because Pilate knew that what was dangerous for the Jewish leaders was eventually, if unchecked, a danger to Rome. This was clearly an uneasy time for the Romans in Palestine. Always aware that at a moment's notice, the people under their control might rebel, it was necessary to keep would-be messiahs in check and under surveillance. This might not be good religious practice, but it was a necessary political and security protocol. The High Priest and the Procurator had a common goal, and that was stability in the province for the sake of both their roles as guardians.

Pontius Pilate served at Caesar's pleasure and the High Priest served Yahweh at the governor's request. When the desires of either Caesar or the governor were not obeyed, Rome would revoke the title, prestige, power and privilege at a moment's notice without courtesy or dignity, as the former High Priest Annas could attest. Both their minds were preoccupied with the delights of status and power, and their hearts distracted by the energy to maintain such honors that they could not hear during the past three days the constant whisper filling the halls of the Fortress Antonia and the Temple precincts . . .

Be Not Afraid!

A particular scent, present in the stone halls of the Roman fortress and along the porticos of the Temple compound was familiar but disconcerting, for these two men, preoccupied with the demands of governing an unruly people, had more important matters to attend to than the whiff of an odor that seemed to surround everything and was everywhere during the last three days of the Nazarene's trial and death. It seeped into the very fabric of the High Priest's garments and the Governor's tunic. They could not escape the scent that clung to their bodies, even though they had attempted several times to bathe the essence away. Instead of a soothing solace, the scent had caused them to become distracted and disturbed.

They were fearful men, afraid of losing and needing to hold onto what they felt was their due and their right. Pilate was intrigued by the Man from Galilee and had bantered with him about the essence of truth, losing the insight and the gift that before him stood the creator of Truth, God Himself. The only truth that Pilate was concerned with was the truth that would preserve his office and his state of affairs in order to please the Emperor, so in gratitude for a job well-done he would reward him with a higher position, perhaps in Rome itself, the center and heart of the world. This backwater province, dirt poor and arrogant before the might and splendor of Rome, found countless ways to disturb the peace and wreak havoc on any career officer that sought a higher place in the Imperial Court. The case of this would-be messiah from Nazareth had pitted the political acumen of these two savvy men of politics and of religion and forced them to conspire, rather than what they preferred, opposing one another. Pilate dreamed of holding office, not in this dismal backyard of the Empire, but craved instead the avenues of Rome and the forums, stadiums, and amphitheaters of a city, envied by the entire known world. Instead Pilate had to deal with zealots and stubborn priests. Above all, he held this Jewish lot in disdain for the privilege accorded them from Rome to worship their God without interference from Roman law or garrison brutes. What was it about this Jewish God that made even a Caesar bend to their demands? Pilate had no such finesse for the diplomacy of religion and often held these Jewish custodians of Torah law in contempt.

Though Pilate feared no gods, be they Roman or Jewish deities, he feared more the loss of power and status and the approval of Caesar than the arbitrary whims of ethereal spirits that interfered with the plans of man. To gain such power and status and to maintain the favor of Caesar who ruled the world, Pilate was not opposed to brutalizing, condemning and torturing any who stood in the path of personal glory. Deaf as he was to the display of mercy and compassion and a heart that beat to a rhythm of love, he could not hear as he rode the paths of Judea the Voice, attempting to soften a cruel heart repeatedly saying ...

Be Not Afraid!

Nor would he allow his heart, hardened by war and mission, to be softened by a fragrance that seemed to permeate the air everywhere, and move his heart to mercy, instead of cold, calculated brutality and violence.

Caiaphas, though not as cruel, possessed a deep devotion to personal gain and title that brought authority, power, respect of the masses, and above all a voice that spoke with the approval of Yahweh. Living as though he were royalty in a palace and accustomed to elegant clothing and fine eating, he would certainly have cringed when Jesus spoke of the rich man and poor Lazarus at his door. It was the Temple and the business of Yahweh that made Caiaphas wealthy and arrogant. Together with his father-in-law, Annas, they controlled Temple worship and the Sanhedrin, and partnered with Pilate to keep the people docile and both spheres of Rome and Jerusalem content and at peace. It was this Rabbi from Galilee that had disrupted such plans and made the people turn from the true worship of Yahweh and believe that a carpenter could be the Anointed One of the Most High.

Such disobedience could not be sanctioned, and to make sure that the people obeyed and followed the Law, it was necessary that one man die so that the nation would survive. That was imperative. Caiaphas would bond with the likes of a lackey of Rome, and together they would prepare a plan to eliminate the danger of the usurper of their power. The fact that the Man they would sacrifice was a Man of purpose, dignity, and right was of little consequence to a governor or a high priest. Blood had to be shed to save their own skins, and the by-product would be a peaceful land with a content Caesar, and the coffers of the

Temple treasury would be rich again with the coins of sacrifice and lawful prayer taxes. Rome would continue to receive unhindered the gold of its conquest and an ordered world. Such were the plans of the men of state and faith, so preoccupied they could not hear the vibrant Voice so clearly state . . .

Be Not Afraid!

Caiaphas was distraught by the events that had unfolded and in that anxious state, his own heart was stressed, and the scent so evident now even in his chambers, began to annoy instead of soothe his troubled heart and conscience.

The unrest was palpable when one of the twelve gave them a cause. The one named Judas would hand this would-be Messiah into their hands, and to capture the One that was causing such distress was too much of an ideal plan to waste, even though it would occur during the Passover Festival. The forces of Rome and the Temple Command would bind together under the guise of a faux holy plan. In a mix of mistruth, arrogance, and deceit, the One who had come to save would die a necessary death so that Rome and Jerusalem would remain in control. The wood of the Cross would seal the deal, and the blood that flowed would be enough to quench the thirst of a maddening crowd. Once he was dead and buried, the dreams of a new world order would diminish, as the Body of the One turned from flesh to ashes. With the stone rolled in place to cover their crime, they posted a guard to make sure that death remained dead, and the Voice that spoke of peace and love would finally be silenced because they would not hear the Voice that proclaimed persistently . . .

Be Not Afraid!

Caiaphas, together with the guards assigned by Pilate to guard a tomb from any devious plans to steal the body and claim a resurrection, was content when the seal was placed upon the stone. From that moment, the scent had pervaded the atmosphere that emitted from the shrouded body, and no matter what measures the High Priest would take, he could not release his own body nor atmosphere from the embrace of the scent annoying and distressing him.

Both men were exceedingly afraid. On this, the third day of a disordered state of affairs when the earth had convulsed and the foundation of the Temple had quaked, and the curtain of the Holy of Holies was rent, there was much confusion throughout the city. Rumors spread far and wide. News of a spectacular nature that distorted the common view for a body was gone and a tomb found empty. Conspiracies were rampart. Many maintained that the disciples stole the body to proclaim a new rite and complete the work of the One now resurrected and freed from the tomb. If that Sunday previous, the people had proclaimed the dead prophet a King and Messiah, what would the people do when they realized that he was now raised from the tomb? What chaos and fear would ensue, and both Caiaphas and Pilate knew that the displeasure of Caesar would destroy their hopes and future and leave them paupers in a land of failure and despair.

Convinced that they would survive if they betrayed the truth and buried again the news that the tomb was empty, they would shroud the truth in the wrappings of deceit, perpetuated by fear. The report that a man dead was now alive would unsettle the world and diminish the gods. An empty tomb would leave the

Temple vacant and the pockets of priests without any gold. This mania must be controlled and the narrative rewritten, so that when the story was told Pilate and Caiaphas would be men of high regard who sought to protect the people from an irrational disease, making the mind rethink the natural order, and would restore the balance of a world that spoke with a Roman voice and believed with a Jewish mind.

This nonsense about resurrection from death to life eroded, not just the hopes of the people but made Yahweh seem petty and pernicious. Protected must they be, so the guards would be bribed to tell other than what was real. They fell asleep; wishing such confusion about coming under the cover of night to steal the body and then claim the dead did rise. How foolish to think that people would believe. This Sunday while the city was in such turmoil, Caiaphas in his palace and Pilate in the Praetorium sat alone and in fear because they refused to believe and hear . . .

Be Not Afraid!

Chapter Thirteen: Restless Dreamer: Claudia

Restless and unable to sleep, Claudia spent the past evenings, not in rest but in disturbed discomfort, tossing and turning all night long. She craved the peace of sleep but to little avail. A bath before bed did little to ease what had become repeated days of chaotic attempts to close her eyes and enter a realm of quiet and calm. Each time she had closed her eyes, she was plagued by dreams that began in calm but turned harsh and difficult to retreat from. In the morning, after fitful sleep and tangled sheets, she would rise anxious, for the dreams turned nightmarish were often so real that they became visible with the dawn. In this somber state of affairs, she entered morning without any peace nor quiet of heart, often imagining that she heard a Voice that offered solace with the words . . .

Be Not Afraid!

But fearful and anxious she was each new morning and carried into the day her dreams and fears of a Man she had not met but was her partner each night, as her head and heart in the subliminal space of night brought her thoughts that moved her nearly to tears. The nightly images were of a Man, known as the Man from Galilee. As the wife of Pilate, she would know and understand the climate of the people that he governed she had become aware of the tenor and the mood of the people as each day she encountered such through her husband Pilate, who ruled as governor over these strange and stubborn people. Unlike her husband who was under Caesar's command, she saw a different land and a people unique, but no different than she or any other

Roman. They were mothers and fathers, sons and daughters, who cared for one another, loved family, and took pride in their history. Like every other people and nation, they considered themselves special. But these people of the Hebrew tribe thought themselves, not just special but chosen by a god that no one could see, but they tried so faultlessly to obey.

Into this distant land far from the splendor of Rome, Claudia had traveled with her husband, the newly appointed governor. He was disappointed with such a lowly post, but she was excited to see the world outside the gates of Rome. Into a cauldron of travel by land and sea, they crossed the desert from the ports of Caesarea and Philippi where they came ashore; she intrigued by the people, the languages, and the faith of the culture. A faith her husband considered barbaric, but she had thought it exotic and interesting.

Claudia, a genteel lady of proper upbringing, came from a wealthy and stately family of Rome. She possessed a gentle heart, a loving spirit, and openness to what the world around her offered. She was curious, yet diligent as a wife and daughter, always faithful to her roots of faith and culture. She was curious to see the world beyond the gates of Rome. Years of childhood stories of peoples and customs in lands conquered by Roman steel had stirred her heart and imagination. She was delighted with the post assigned by Caesar to be among the people called Chosen. She had taken time to read the scrolls of this ancient and venerable people that her husband called zealots and traitors to Rome, but she knew otherwise for they possessed a gift of wisdom and spiritual insight.

To her husband, this was just a task and a movement up the ladder to fame and fortune. It would be several years before he would return to the center of power, and in the meantime Pilate would make a name for himself so that even from this distant land, Caesar would hear of his renown. Little did Claudia and Pilate realize that the fame Pilate sought would come at a deep cost. His name would be known throughout the ages, not for greatness but for the betrayal of truth, and would fall into infamy and disrepute. The wife, aware that something was amiss on that fateful Friday that the world would later call Good Friday, was disturbed and distressed. When a Cross was raised upon Golgotha, not in her sight but in her dreams, and the Man to die upon that tree she recognized as the Man from Galilee. Unknown to her husband, Claudia had heard this Man speak in the porticos of the Temple before that Sunday when he was proclaimed a king and the forces of politics and faith were turned against him.

He had spoken of love and forgiveness, and her heart had craved to hear more. She was intrigued by the stories about healing the lame, cleansing the lepers, and feeding the multitudes. Claudia wanted to see this Man that caused the High Priest and her husband such concern and grief. He had passed by one day beneath the fortress that served as the garrison for the seat of Roman power as he was on his way to the Temple compound so that he could pray and then teach. His teachings her husband and the High Priest claimed were subversive to Rome and a reason to monitor his movements and those they called his disciples and followers. The members of the Jewish authority tried often to trap him and thus accuse him of religious impiety and blasphemy to settle the score. At each junction, the Man from Galilee would trump their charge, and the number of his disciples would continue to grow, as did the concerns of Pilate and Caiaphas.

When Claudia did see the Man, she was unimpressed by his demeanor but his eyes she saw and the words that she heard mesmerized her, as she mulled his wisdom within her mind. She recalled that day not so long ago when he had walked the path that passed her view and glanced in her direction. As their eyes engaged, she breathed in a fragrance so pure and pleasing that it sparked a remembrance in her dreams, and she heard his Voice so loud and clear . . .

Be Not Afraid!

From that first moment when their eyes met, the pages of history turned so quickly and completely. The days ran into one another so that from day to day one could not tell the score. Pilate, infuriated with the antics of would-be messiahs and any hint of rebellion, kept a strong arm braced with the support of troops on the back of this stiff-necked people who were always looking for an excuse to riot and turn to mayhem. The High Priest agitated the calm by insisting that a Rabbi could turn the serenity of Passover into a storm of revolt. Sad to say, it would be the celebration of Passover that would ignite the tinderbox of zealous faith, Roman sensitivity, and the plans of an unseen God, as the people remembered the saving power of Yahweh and yearned for him to renew such this day. Renew, Yahweh would, but would use a governor and a high priest to complete the plan, as it unfolded from the dreams of a governor's wife to the halls of power and the Temple of prayer, and end upon a hill, remembered as Calvary. Claudia wondered what fate awaited the Man she held nightly in her dreams, with the words echoing in her ears . . .

Be Not Afraid!

On that day they first met within the space of sight and hearing, she had monitored the movements of this Man of prayer. She heard about the confusion caused when this Man of peace challenged the money changers and sellers of sacrificial animals and accused them of being less than pious and reverent, sending them scurrying with their coins and animals from the Temple. As if this would not be enough to be noticed by those in power, there were rumors and gossip that a man had been raised from the dead. This was no tall tale but an authentic miracle, witnessed by many of noble and true birth, for the man, Lazarus, was a friend of the Man from Galilee and well-known and respected by many of the same repute from the city of Jerusalem and beyond. How could one deny that once dead for four days, he was seen by many to be alive and well by eyewitnesses whose testimony no court could deny. But the Governor and High Priest were unmoved and gave in to the expediency of the moment and would arrest a good Man, for they could not hear as Claudia had, so finely attuned was she to the whisper, and the Voice that uttered . . .

Be Not Afraid!

It happened so quickly. The Passover was being celebrated, and then word spread throughout the night that they had arrested the Rabbi who had been betrayed by his own. Betrayed and then denied, as those he had called friend took flight and so securely hid. Trials and rumors of charges flew through the night. With unsubstantiated evidence, the Sanhedrin met under the cover of night. Accusations of blasphemy and rebellion were leveled at the Man of Peace, but it was unclear if any of the charges would adhere. On that fateful night, the oil and lights burned way into the night both in the rooms of the Governor and High Priest, but also in the room of a wife and daughter who could not sleep. At early morning dawn, she sent word to her husband who was in command, "Have nothing to do with this Man, for my dreams have been plagued by restless spirits that disturbed my night. Abandon this course and set this Man free." Claudia, who usually stayed far beyond the scope of politics where men command, this night was moved and fortified by a dream that was clear and a Voice that said . . .

Be Not Afraid!

The message was delivered, and Pilate read the plea from the woman whose intuition he came to fear. He thus sought to follow through on what her dreams had produced, but he was torn between comfort and what was the truth. In the end, he tried to release the Man he knew was innocent of any crime but would commit him to the tree to die because a crowd had cried out in such a loud voice. The letter he had read from Claudia would be tossed aside, and the man she loved as her husband and friend would this day cleanse his hands of any grime, but they would never be pure in the end, for Claudia would always hear in the stillness of the night and in her dreams at twilight, "He suffered under Pontius Pilate, was crucified, died and was buried." From this Friday onward, Pilate's nights would be restless and plagued by dreams of this Man, dead but ever present, while Claudia would sleep contentedly

Days of chaos and confusion continued to swirl around this city of saints and sinners, and then this incredible news reached Pilate and Claudia that a tomb, once sealed was wide open. The body secured, sealed, and wrapped in a shroud, was nowhere to be found. She wondered what this all meant, as she unexpectedly breathed in the fragrance she recalled from when the Man was in the flesh, and suddenly the room was aglow and she was aware this was no dream, but the moment was so real that she cried out for the Master who responds . . .

Be Not Afraid!

Chapter Fourteen: A Doubter
No More: Thomas

Before the others could be roused from their sleep, Thomas, known as Didymus, which literally meant twin, collected his sparse belongings and prepared to leave the Upper Room without waking the others who continued to sleep, as this new day of Sunday began to dawn. The past three days had been nightmarish and frightful, not just for him but for all the followers of the Master. It seemed, just like yesterday when they were beginning the journey to Jerusalem for the celebration of the Passover, their mood already gloomy for Jesus had told them he was going to Jerusalem to die. He knew that not everyone lives forever, and the time would come when all are called by death to leave this life and await the resurrection of the dead. They had been arguing as they were walking about who would be the greatest in this kingdom that the Master was planning to create. When he had asked what they were discussing and arguing about, they felt embarrassed, for it seemed so petty. The only one who seemed to have any perspective about the purpose and meaning for the trip to Jerusalem was Jesus, and here they were making almost a mockery of his heaviness of heart, as he knew then what this journey would entail. It would mean the Master's death. Ever since the raising of Lazarus from the dead and the scene with the moneychangers in the Temple, Jesus was not a welcome sight in the Holy City. He had a tendency to set the religious leaders on edge, and the Romans were always nervous when would-be messiahs made the rounds, especially during Passover.

Nerves were on edge, and Jesus was the reason, and yet with purpose and determination, his sights set on that Holy City that often was responsible for the killing of prophets. If he had to wager a bet, Jesus was one of those whom the residents of this city would certainly consider a problem and a danger. But to kill him, that he was so sure could never be. He even boasted that he and the others would journey with him to Jerusalem in order to die with him. What bravado and hubris! He was one of the first to run when the guards came that night in the garden to arrest Jesus. In fact, they all ran that night. How shameful and disgraceful, to leave the Master behind with the thugs that had captured him, when one of their own had betrayed him into their hands. Not one of them had the right to judge Judas; they had all betrayed the Master by their feet racing in the opposite direction, covered not in dignity, but scurrying away in fear. These were the thoughts that played out in the mind and heart of Thomas over and over these three nights. Hidden and locked behind the doors were all twelve, assembled to share that fateful night. Even now, Thomas could see the remains of that meal still on the table. What a Passover indeed it was! Thomas recalled that at a point in the Passover ritual, Jesus had stopped and done something that caught them all by surprise. He got up from the table, and taking a bowl, pitcher, and towel, Jesus, Lord and Master had knelt and washed the feet of each of the apostles in that room. Such an act should be carried out by a slave but was performed by the Master. The apostles were speechless. The act, when completed, had added a new dimension to the mission and message of the Master, who said it was what he expected each of us to do for one another. Imagine playing and then acting the slave and servant for another. How utterly undivine, but supremely Godly. Such a simple act, Jesus had raised to a level of dignity that even as Thomas saw the bowl and the pitcher, his own heart sank in shame for missing the message and running to save his own neck. In racing out of the garden into the safety of the city, those newly washed feet were soiled once again after being cleansed by the very hands of the One who lay dead in a tomb. Quietly, Thomas passed the remains on that table and sensed a scent that was pleasing but also a reminder of his behavior that was less than manly and sorely cowardly. With determination, newly regained, he focused on that door that needed to be unbarred to set him free from the agony of these days of death and grief. So much he was determined to run that he could not hear the whisper that embraced him as he opened the door . . .

Be Not Afraid!

He closed the door quietly behind him and raced down the stairs and hopefully into the oblivion of obscurity. If he only had waited a few more moments, he would have engaged the women who were racing back from the tomb. The original journey to Jerusalem, where he had claimed he would be willing to die with Christ, had all but been forfeited as he fled the city that had once again claimed the life of a prophet. Their paths would never cross this day, but as Thomas left the city as he rushed out, hoping and praying his flight was undetected by any guards or disciples, and so he missed the most spectacular news that

Magdala brought to the Upper Room. Willing as he was just a few days ago to journey to this city to die if he must with the Master, he was fleeing the city, with his head bowed and covered by a hood to offer protection against prying eyes, by the same gate the Master had used when he journeyed upon a colt to the acclaim of the populace and the cries of "Messiah" and "Hosanna." But there were no 'Hosannas" this morning; only images of fright and flight, and so fast were his feet moving along the way, he passed two disciples walking to Emmaus in disappointment, distraught for all the dreams had disappeared. Such dreams about a kingdom and a reign of peace were long dispersed, as the Man who had proclaimed such words laid cold and dead, turning to ashes and disappearing, as were his words and the hopes of all who had believed. If only Thomas, as he passed the two men had slowed to greet them, he too would have met the One they were so sore distressed about. But racing past them, he gave not a backward glance as he believed they were followers of the One they all mourned, and in his own flight to safety he could not turn and greet the others in a normal tone for fear they might delay his departure, so gripped was he by this unnatural fear. That fear, a whisper he heard again, repeating what he had heard before . . .

Be Not Afraid!

But he was afraid and passed the two without noticing them and overtaking them on the road, not to Emmaus where a miracle awaited but to a town of no note to disappear and to rescue his life from this towering despair. The images plague him both day and night, as he raced out of this horrid city on such a sunny day in hopes of outmaneuvering the nightmarish sights, embedded in his mind, and his heart ached for the crime he had committed. That crime weighed so heavily upon his life that his breathing was impaired, and his sight blurred. If it were not for the smooth surface of the road, he would have stumbled and fallen, injured not physically, but in his spirit that despairs. He remembered that Last Meal and the words that the Master had uttered: "This is My Body, and this is My Blood." It was a new ritual and a new form for he had proclaimed a new covenant, truly written in his blood. A sacrifice and a theology proclaimed by the beams of a Cross, bound together not by savagery but by Love. In the fear that overcame them in the garden and then in the Upper Room, they could not see past the reality of death and the horror of suffering that led Thomas and the others to flee the scene, and Love was left alone and captured to be hanged upon a tree.

Rabbis and teachers had never imagined that the God who had given the Law and saved the people would allow the Son to die so ignominiously, fastened to the wood and bleeding so that God could heal a world gone mad with pride and brutality. The images and scenes were blazing in his mind, as Thomas raced to a place where the images would no longer haunt him, and the others would not find him. And yet, as the Stranger in White approached the pair on the road to Emmaus, and a woman, who had been forgiven much, reached the Cenacle with an astounding tale, Thomas was preoccupied and distracted, still unable to hear a reassuring and confident Voice saying . . .

Be Not Afraid!

A week had gone by, and no matter what he did, Thomas could not erase the image of the Man hanging so distressfully upon the wood of the Cross. His heart, instead of being freed from such fear, was heavier because of the weight of such devotion that crippled him and made him despair. Even in this remote part of the Promised Land, news of a remarkable kind made its way to be heard throughout almost all of the land. Jesus, the Man they had crucified, many claimed they had seen and was alive. Pilate and Caiaphas were in a confused and dangerous state, as the people continued to be enthralled by a Man, now more powerful dead than he was alive. They conspired to no avail about how to kill the Man, already dead and buried. The message and memory of the Man now had substance and life, gathering all those who had seen and believed into a new family. The apostle, Thomas, once so well known, could not hide undetected from the Love that had called him three years earlier. Words of incredible sightings of the Man thought dead left the apostle in a quandary, and he asked himself, "Must I now journey back to Jerusalem?" The answer in his heart was an affirming "yes," and stunned relatives who had offered him solace and safety were puzzled by this turn of events. Upon the same road that he had just walked to escape, he turned back in the direction he had just fled, so as to return and listen to the Voice, growing louder and firmer with each step . . .

Be Not Afraid!

He approached the city, confident and with less fear, he had a swagger and a bravado that had escaped him earlier. Upon entering the Upper Room, he found all the apostles talking at once so he could barely make out what they were saying. "We have seen the Lord!" By stubborn will and unfolding grace, he, maintained his demeanor and would not bend to hysteria or fear,

Unless he could see for himself the person all claimed to have seen, and unless he could touch the wounds himself, he would never believe. Such a statement from one of the Master's own sent a shiver through the room because it bordered on a new type of blasphemy. There was no convincing the man who was an apostle and had made a statement on his price for belief. It might not be the silver of Judas or the words of denial from the man who was fervent in his conviction that he had seen the Lord. He would not be so petty in what he expected, but to see the wounds and to touch them that would be his price. While they argued and complained and tried to bring one another to a calmer frame of mind, the room filled with a strange light and a fragrance that permeated the room. A bowl on the floor began to vibrate, and the bread still on the table from that Passover night was bathed in a remarkable glow as the apostles were filled with delight and Thomas began to experience unease and fright. With the doors barred and locked, Jesus the Man, all in white and light, entered the room, saying to all now silent...

Be Not Afraid!

The apostles were in sheer delight, while Thomas clung to the wall, not in fright but in hopes of not being noticed. In spite of all the surrounding joy in the room Thomas was in a state of gloom. He thought to himself, how was this possible, and why had he not believed them when they told him this incredible news. While his mind raced in confusion, he heard the Master's voice, so clear and encouraging for him to come near. With head bowed and lips trembling, not out of fear but in deep regret, the tears welled in his eyes and were shed down his face. As once Peter had understood the feeling of such sorrow Thomas was experiencing, Peter revisited that moment when the Master had so appeared, bringing the one who had denied him to tears. He shared once again the grief he had shed and knew what Thomas must be feeling for the unbelief he had voiced. And the Lord in dazzling light called him to come forward to see and feel. With his head still bowed, he could not move, not because of fear but from shame and guilt. Peter nudged him to go forward, and he did so with a gentle smile. The Lord gazed at him and greeted him with a smile and the words, spoken directly to Thomas but for all to hear,

Be Not Afraid!

The words were spoken, and feeling their effects, he moved closer to the Lord, who stretched out his hands for Thomas to touch. Thomas, however, was so ashamed that he could not allow himself this act so brazen and bold for one who had expressed his disbelief. The hands were outstretched, but the apostle, now humbled, fell to his knees, almost in ecstasy, and acclaimed a creed of belief so brief but in clarity, professing, "My Lord and My God . . ."

And Thomas was no longer afraid!

Chapter Fifteen: A Changed Man: Barabbas

He staggered along the streets during the early morning hours of this, the first day of the week. He still felt that he was somehow in a dream state, for how could this be possible? He was here alive and well while a Rabbi lay dead and buried. Three days ago he was a marked and condemned man, subject to the power of Rome and the cruelty of execution. Today, he was a free man, allowed to walk where he would, do as he wished, and say what he desired. Since that most incredible day when the heavens had rained down their displeasure, the earth had rocked and rumbled, and the people had fled to their homes in terror because of what had transpired, he was a nearly condemned man, left alone and unattended by guards, to make his way along the muddy path that led to the city gate of Jerusalem. He glanced over his back, and he could see the three crosses, covered in the downpour of rain with the backdrop of lightning and thunder. Upon the Cross in the center, he could make out the frame of the Man who had taken his place upon that tree. Who would have thought that such a day of freedom for him would leave another broken and dead and a city reeling in fear. Barabbas tried to make sense out of the events that had occurred in this city of prophets, but his head was a little too groggy from an overload of wine over the last two nights. A free spirit, he was drinking in the vigor of pleasures and sights he was free to experience, and so he did. In such a state of uneasy steps and a foggy head, he thought he heard a voice and stopped to listen more attentively, and he thought he heard a Voice speak...

Be Not Afraid!

He turned to see who had spoken, but no one was there. He continued his journey quickly back into the city where he had spent the last two days in jubilant celebration, for the cares of the world no longer plagued him. The yoke of imprisonment had been lifted from the neck that a Roman foot had attempted to crush but could not because the people had spoken, "Free Barabbas, free Barabbas!" He could hear the shouts that called his name so he would be set free and the other would die upon the tree. He asked a question that thirty-three years earlier another had asked that would link these two lives to eternity and the story of salvation, unfolding upon that hill they called Golgotha . . .

"How can this be? I, a revolutionary am set free, while the Rabbi, Prophet, and Healer is made to bear the wood and grasp the nails." He shivered, as his mind returned to that moment when he had stood on that Praetorium step and faced the crowd, wild with hate he thought had been meant for him until he had spied the other Man, disfigured and bloodied, and it was for him they cried, not for mercy but for vengeance. Barabbas felt a twinge of pity for the criminal with whom he was set in a contest to see who would win and be set free, while the other would die ignominiously. The cries began first with a shout and then a torrent of loud and abrasive voices, clamoring for the beast to run wild while the sheep was to be slaughtered in grim style. The crowd became a blistering mob, screeching and searing with vile words, the very Word made Flesh. With his head bowed before the festering wound of humanity, the One who had come to heal was put on trial and found guilty. Barabbas could not believe his own ears, nor trust his eyes as he surveyed the crowd. Were they calling for his name instead of that of the humble and gentle Rabbi? It was not a dream but maybe it was a cruel hoax by a devious Roman mind, playing a trick on such an unsuspecting person. But there in full view, Pilate and his soldiers were moving to unbind the chains that held him fast. With disdain, they released the one they had hoped to burden with the cross and to enjoy a game as they mocked and abuse him to receive retribution for the killing that he had been judged with committing and to the gibbet he should have gone.

The soldiers were not pleased as they released this man, a criminal and murderer, who had used his strength, not for good but to inflict upon the Roman overlords a tax, not in silver or gold, but in the Roman blood of their own comrades in arms, who had given their lives to maintain supreme over this land and indigenous people.

They released this brute and were left with just this Man. Angry, their blood sport unpaid. They demanded a price and this Rabbi would do for the moment. As the crowd, pleased with their demands to see the criminal released to play in this cruel drama, and the One who is Truth treated with false regard and violent savagery. Amid the shouting of the people, the soldiers were angry, and the priests and scribes, delighted, with the outcome preconceived but shocking nonetheless, barely notice the pitcher and water as Pilate washed his hands of this innocent blood. In all this barbaric and gross noise, the host of people were deaf to the Voice trying to calm by speaking…

Be Not Afraid!

Released, Barabbas was pushed down the stairs and directly entered the mob and became a friend and new son. Racing to make sure they did not change their minds about this most uncommon release, he turned to look gleefully at the soldiers who were seething because of this surrender of Roman superiority, but he cast a look in the direction of the Man, so mournfully directed to another space to be mocked and then led out to be crucified. The Man's eyes for just a moment were raised, and he stared directly into, not just the eyes but the very heart of the rebellious zealot who was determined to escape deeper into the crowd but is haunted by those eyes and heard in the midst of the mob a Voice, saying . . .

Be Not Afraid!

That look, that stare, those eyes, the piercing glance that would hold his attention these many days past. No matter where he might run or roam, he could not hide from those eyes. He saw the Cross, cast in such a radiant light, and then a peculiar smell was heavy in the air, but pleasing to the senses. Barabbas was never acquainted with the genteel style of living of fresh smells, clean air, and fragrant scents. His was a rough and gritty life that held little that was sweet or pleasing, but what was that sweet aroma, caressing his mind and heart and embracing his body, that he believed for a moment it was a Roman plan to make sure he turned mad. Through the gate, he rushed to escape the Light and the scent, but realized that both cling to wherever he was going, and in a moment, terrifying yet peaceful, this penetrating Light that nearly blinds him, making him unable to see, absorbed him. Rubbing his eyes as he sought his bearing, so as not to stumble and fall, he rested awkwardly against the frame of a nearby house and heard the Voice, saying . . .

Be Not Afraid! ...

Suddenly, he recognized the Man who was standing before him, all aglow. It is the One who surely was dead, the One that took his place upon the Cross. How was it, he wondered, that he stands before him in body, but still the wounds can clearly be seen. Hands bruised and red marks imparted by the nails. The head of the One he recalled was so bowed was now framed with an indelible smile, and his entire frame was bathed, not in pain but in joyful ecstasy. "How can this be? What trick is this?" the rebel proclaimed. He wondered if he had been poisoned by some Roman treachery that had played magic with the mind.

The Light came closer, and the Man raised His hand, not in violence but in a strange gesture that made Barabbas feel at peace as he heard and believed the Voice as it said...

Be Not Afraid!

Chapter Sixteen: To the Mount and a Commission

Forty days had come and gone since the Rising of the Lord was made known, and the apostles and disciples had seen the Lord. Days and nights when there had been visits and apparitions. People in many numbers had seen the Lord, risen and living. They attested, witnessed, and proclaimed that they had seen the Lord. Simon the fisherman, who once had denied him and had raced from village and town to swim in the sea, just to be with him and tell others of this remarkable sight that One dead had come back to life. At each visit, the moments they had spent together, the Lord had begun and ended with the words . . .

Be Not Afraid!

His Presence was comforting. They craved to be near him. They no longer cowered in shame or fear, knowing that at the moment he had needed them most, they had all disappeared. But there was forgiveness, when he first appeared. He shared his new Life and Light with the men he had loved most to bring them back from the death of the soul and the darkness of night. They had been freed and made whole by his appearances. The wounds were the reminder of Love, not guilt; the Light, a reassurance of comfort and hope, and the breath of a new season of grace touching their hearts and bringing them a joy they never knew, delighting to be in such awesome company. They were content until the day they were called forth to meet him at the Mount in Bethany, perhaps thinking he would set forth the plan to make the Kingdom real, and they excitedly wanted to hear his design.

Singing psalms and recounting the time they had first met the Lord, when upon the Sea of Galilee, he first called Andrew and then in turn found his brother, Simon, to bring to the Lord. Who could forget the brothers, John and James, the ones they called the sons of thunder.

These fishermen, the Master passed and called to them to come and follow, and they did. And Levi, who was called Matthew, was so interested in the coins that he had stacked in perfect symmetry and relished their gleam, sparking his soul, but one day the Master passed the customhouse where this man of taxes was working, and the look the Master gave him caused those coins to tumble and lose their shine. He left that place posthaste to offer a dinner to the Lord and to make amends for a life that was disgraced but the Lord had raised him up higher than any bag of gold could and gave him a place far finer to store his treasures, and that would be in heaven. Then, there was Nathaniel, called by the name, Bartholomew. What was more important than names was that Jesus had called him a faithful man, one without guile. If only the Lord could see deep within each of us, what virtues would he find and what nickname would he give? Instead of being pleased, this man brought to the Lord insisted on asking, "How do you know me?" In simple style Jesus explained, "I saw you beneath the fig tree," and Nathaniel perceived there was indeed a prophet, even if from Nazareth. Each thus far heard the words, "Come and follow me," and so each did. But the group was yet complete, for others were to be called.

Thomas, the one called the twin, was a favorite because he said what was in his heart in expressing his incredible disbelief at the moment of heaven's greatest moment. He became our best defense when the forces of doubt would cloud our vision, and we needed to hear and believe the words that Christ speaks to us even today . . .

Be Not Afraid!

This unique crew of no special character but much vice, the Lord called to come and serve with a willing heart and a soul open to the power of grace. Into this mix of sinners and saints, of devil and angel, there were others of no great repute, but the Gospel and their blood would make their names immortal as they dared to preach the impossible and to proclaim a Truth without credit that Love conquered death, and a baby could be God in our midst. These ordinary and impractical men would be touched by divinity, so that they proclaimed Mystery, for the Master called them to Come and Follow Me!

Philip was called to become part of a strange band of musicians of the heart and a symphony of God that would use instruments of grace, conducted by the Lord in the lyrics and tones of hope and joy. These men, called by the Lord, would sing with their testimony of Truth, joining with the songs of countless men and women in singing songs of love throughout the ages. However, before this song might be sung, the instruments played, and the symphony prepared, others must be called to complete this chorus group that would live forever until the end of time, chanting the lines of salvation and redemption that would stand the test of time, "Christ has died, Christ is

Risen, Christ will come again!" Philip would bring to the Lord the one who had some loaves and fishes and this little offering to feed thousands. It would be Philip who would give voice to the dream, and show us the Father, with the response being, "If you see me, you have seen the Father, for we are One! A simple request and a theological release, setting the stage for the Trinity, and faith and doctrine would embrace for the ages.

To this sacred band would be placed in an immortal stance, James the Younger and James the Great. One would become the leader of Jerusalem during those early times and forfeit his head and life for the Lord whose Presence and words he awaited upon this mount they called Bethany. To this gathering of apostles and disciples, we saw the man called James the Younger, whose words and witness would find evidence in the letter bearing his name. James would urge us to be faithful followers of Christ. "Be doers of the Word, and not merely hearers."

To this gathering awaiting the Lord upon the Mount, we saw Simon the Zealot. A man passionate for all that was Israel and the Law, and whose life and words would preach the New Law. Meeting the Lord and becoming part of the inner core of followers, his heart, hardened to do harm and violence, would soften at seeing a vision of a kingdom, not of this world but a Kingdom of God, where all were sons and daughters of the Father that Jesus had come to reveal. He stood here upon this mount, awaiting the Lord who had summoned them to come. They were called to come and follow, and so they did, sometimes not exactly as the Lord preferred, but patient he was and Master to them all as a Teacher and Guide.

Missing from this clan of the ordinary and the sinner who struggled to believe was the one whose very life was lost upon a halter hung from a tree. On that fateful Friday, future generations would call Good, this man, Judas, could not allow himself to be embraced by the mercy of God, and so in despair he rendered his heart from the tree of life and fell into an abyss of nothingness, as we wonder whether tears were shed for a life so lost.

These men, called and blessed by the Lord who suddenly appeared in their midst. Forty days since that Sunday that distorted the meaning of life, Jesus would appear to Simon Peter and to many others both day and night. He would come in their midst and proclaim to all a message of peace, reminding them in person...

Be Not Afraid!

Now arrayed in the splendor of light, the Man whom they have come to know, love and adore, was about to leave them. Before the Christ did so, he reminded them all and in turn us that he is with us always and even to the end of time. They should not be afraid, for he and the Father would send a Helper, one who would be an Advocate and Guide to lead them to places the Lord would ultimately decide. He was explicit not to leave the city of Jerusalem, but to await the One that would be sent to shoulder their burdens and help with their plans. Such a force would be needed for this incredible saga to be fruitful and expand. Unsure what was about to transpire, for the time since the tomb had been found empty had been days of more than mere adventure but incredible moments, when the Divine had become real and the human refined. The apostles and those who were mere witnesses for these forty days and nights sometimes could not venture to give language to the most remarkable news of death having been conquered and the world restored to life. The balance that for eons had been out of sorts was placed in synchronized harmony by the Blood and the Cross, but that was just one facet of the Divine and Noble plan, not just to seek death as a restitution but the empty tomb as a resurrected creation restored, renewed and reborn.

The plan, conceived and carried forth by a command of will, made so in the flesh of the Son who had endured and restored the manner of life that God, whose name means I AM, had brokered and destroyed the power of hell. Upon this Mount, the Lord had breathed forth life with a new command, "Go forth to all the lands, and preach the Good News and baptize all in the name of the Father, the Son, and the Holy Spirit." As they listened intently, they perceived something amiss, for as he spoke and they listened, he was ascending right before their eyes into the clouds, and the heavens opened to receive the One that the Father had sent forth to heal and make holy all that they saw. Gazing at one another in disbelief that once dead and now alive, they see him before their eyes vanish without any trace, and feel abandoned, orphaned in this space, with the Voice of their Master, saying loud enough so all hear . . .

Be Not Afraid!

Pentecost: The Spirit Abounds

Together with Mary, the Mother of Jesus, the apostles and the faithful disciples remain gathered in the room of the Last Supper. Since the day when he had been lifted from their sight, they followed Jesus' command and stayed within the walls of Jerusalem, awaiting the One whom Jesus and the Father would usher forth. In prayer and sacred conversation, they waited, abiding in this time the Presence of the Lord that they had come to know and understand in the breaking of the bread. Eyes might not see nor minds truly perceive, but they all recalled how he had said at that Last Supper to all those present, "Do this in memory of me." And so they did, night after night, assembling first in prayer and then in the dialogue of faith to recall his teachings and what was said. First, Peter and then another apostle would stand and recall a moment in the life of this group who had traveled from city and town, proclaiming and healing and preparing for this moment.

They broke the bread and drank from the cup and they could feel His Presence, if not in the flesh but in the Spirit, passionate and real, vibrant and living, physical and spiritual, and fully the Lord. Each sip from the cup and each taste of the bread, they savored, witnessing to the marvelous gift only the mind of God could have conceived. "Take and eat; this is my Body; take and drink for this is my Blood." They know but cannot fully understand the meaning and depth of this Mystery of faith, so they simply said, "Amen." In that moment they became what they consumed, a new family and community where God is the Father, and each a child of the One they praised, for the Son now raised, brought all his followers to the Father who embraced them as sons and daughters welcome to enter the Kingdom and walk into the Promised Land. Before the sustenance of such food was able to bear fruit, they needed to do what the Lord commanded: to preach and baptize and make all nations one. How could they fully grasp the quandary of choices of how this should be done. They still had shadows of fears and doubts plaguing them and causing them to develop amnesia as they failed to remember what the Lord had told them.

In the midst of this confusion, surrounded by prayer, they experienced a movement unlike any they understood. There was a whirling of wind that was anything but gentle, but loud and all consuming, it devoured the house and all within, and the wind was such that no door or shutters could contain it. Into this maelstrom, there appeared a gush, not just of wind but also of fire that rested upon each head. The wind, stronger in force than any mere storm, and enveloped the room and all within. The fire danced above each head but did not consume. In a burst of light with fire mixed with the wind, there was a calm that each man and woman experienced. It was more than just an emotion, but a mystical experience that would shape all their hearts to accept instinctively what the Lord had revealed. There was no fear and no longer any doubts but courage grew fast and swift as the wind subsided.

In a flash, Peter was up from the floor and racing to the doors, unbarring and then opening them to reveal a multitude of people who had heard and come to explore this remarkable noise. Peter, to the acclaim of many, began to proclaim to all assembled the Good News to be heard, and as he began to proclaim Jesus as Lord, there was heard within the Upper Room a Voice, uttering in grand fashion and jubilation,

Be Not Afraid!

Acknowledgments

It is necessary to thank a number of people who have been inspirational and encouraging as this work of faith and heart came into this created form of prose and images.

Deep appreciation to my readers: Gloria Petrone, Barbara Consorte, Father Larry Lewis, MM and Elizabeth Skolnick. Special thanks for their suggestions.

With thanks for the encouragement of Brother David Migliorino, OSF and those of Notre Dame Regional High School.

Special thanks and appreciation go to the students of Notre Dame Regional High School who shared their time and talent so that the chapters of this book could be enriched with their art. In particular I wish to thank the following students: Claudia Albuixech-Robinson, Mindy Diebold, Miranda Menz, Elizabeth Raines, Theresa Vercide, Adeline Vowels and Livia Wunderlich.

A word of thanks is given to the Secular Franciscans who by their prayers and fraternity have been a constant source of support and encouragement.

Special thanks to Brother Mark Waldmann, OSF whose tech savvy has offered incalculable advice regarding the inner realm of the computer and program uses including the shortcuts.

CPSIA information can be obtained
at www.ICGtesting.com
Printed in the USA
BVHW091927240419
546406BV00009B/373/P